Blockchain

Ultimate guide to understanding blockchain, bitcoin, cryptocurrencies, smart contracts and the future of money.

Written by Mark Gates

Blockchain: Ultimate guide to understanding blockchain, bitcoin, cryptocurrencies, smart contracts and the future of money.

First edition. June 1, 2017.

Written by Mark Gates.

Errors

Please Contact Us If You Find Any Errors

While every effort is taken to ensure the quality and accuracy of this book. Spelling, grammar and other errors are often missed in the early versions of publication.

We appreciate you contacting us first if you noticed any errors in this book before taking any other action. This allows us to quickly fix these errors before it negatively impacts the author.

If you find any issues or errors with this book, please contact us and we'll correct these as soon as possible.

Readers that notify us of errors will be invited to receive advance reader copies of future books published.

Errors: errors@wisefoxpub.com

Reviews and Feedback

Reviews and feedback help improve this book and help the author.
If you enjoy this book, it would be greatly appreciated if you were able to take a few moments to share your opinion and post a review on Amazon. Even just a rating and a few words would help a lot.

A shortened link to help you leave a review is below:
www.wisefoxpub.com/blockchain

For any general feedback about the book, please feel free to contact us at the email address below:

Feedback: contact@wisefoxpub.com

Bonus Blockchain Resource Guide

Get the free Blockchain resource guide in digital format.

The guide includes the glossary of terms from this book in digital format.

It also includes continuously updated resources to learn more about Blockchain, Bitcoin, Ethereum and ICOs.

You can get the guide from the link below:
www.wisefoxbooks.com/resources

Table of Contents

Introduction

"On the internet, nobody knows you're a dog." - Peter Steiner

"On the blockchain, nobody knows you're a fridge." - Richard Gendal Brown

Blockchain technology has been called the greatest innovation since the internet.
Proponents of the technology claim it will disrupt every industry that exists today and impact the lives of almost everybody on the planet within a few decades.

Is blockchain technology one of the greatest technological revolutions in history or is it just hype?

Will blockchain technology cause governments and banking systems to change the way they process information or will it be business as usual?

Are the evangelists of blockchain technology companies too excited and creating another tech bubble in what is essentially just a new way to create a database?

In this book, we'll look at the answers to these questions as well as address the different arguments for and against blockchain technology.

This book will explain what blockchain technology is, how it works, and the potential uses along with the impact of the technology.

While it will cover a lot of the potential applications and benefits, it is not a book that will solely evangelize blockchain technology as the answer to all the problems in governments, banking systems or industries.

The aim is to provide a balanced understanding of blockchain technology combining the benefits and potential uses with the risks, disadvantages and addressing some of the hype around it.

This book is written for people new to blockchain technology looking for a non-technical understanding of the technology. There are some technical aspects covered towards the end of the book; however, the technical details of the blockchain are not the focus of the book.

When first learning about blockchain technology, I found there was a lot of technical information about blockchain technology scattered and poorly structured, but no clear guide starting from a non-technical basis.

I have written this book as it is the book I wanted to read when first learning about and trying to understand the blockchain.

I hope you enjoy reading this book and find it useful, educational, and insightful in your understanding of blockchain technology.

Notes about key points:

- At the end of each chapter there are key points, these will repeat the information in the chapter in short dot points. This is for people that would prefer to get summarized information of key points.

- If you are not enjoying a chapter or don't have time to read it, feel free to skip to the key points to get the main information from the chapter.

- The key points will also help with note taking, revision of material or quickly finding material to reference it later without having to read the entire chapter again.

- If you have read the entire chapter, you can skip the key points as it may seem repetitive of the material already read.

Chapter One: What is the blockchain?

To put it simply, a blockchain is like a database; it's a way of storing records of value and transactions.

Unfortunately, that simple definition won't excite people and will leave many people thinking "So what? All that hype for a new type of database?"

However, calling blockchain a new type of database is like saying email is a new way of sending people letters. While the blockchain is a database, that definition doesn't explain the true genius behind how the blockchain stores records of value and transactions.

In the past when any asset of value or transaction was recorded in a database, people relied on a third party like a bank, government or company to record this information. People trust that banks won't steal their money as the government regulates them. If a bank fails, people trust that the government will ensure their deposits of money are safe.

When transferring money or paying for goods and services, people trust credit card companies and banks will take the correct amount from their bank account and deposit it into the account of the seller. The seller trusts that the credit card company will pay them the money and if there is any dispute or fraud on the transaction it will be handled through the credit card company.

If a buyer at a store is paying with cash, the seller trusts that they can take this piece of paper with a number on it that is backed by the government to another store and exchange it to pay for other goods and services. The sellers also trust that if they take the note to a bank, they can convert it into a digital cash balance in their bank account that can be used to pay for purchases using credit cards or online transactions.

People trust these external institutions with their money and information. People trust the credit card companies and banks will keep their credit card details private and safe. They trust that the credit card companies and banks have databases with records of their balances and transactions that are accurately maintained. The banks trust that the governments have databases and records of the notes issued.

This trust in institutions is not just financial but extends to every area of our life. If you've ever borrowed a book from a library, the library maintains a database of all the books they have. The library also maintains a database of members, all the books that have been borrowed, the date each book is to be returned, and any books that are overdue.

The library maintains a central database of your personal details, home address, and information. If you don't return a book you have borrowed, they can send you fines, and if required they could take legal action against you for theft.

Those database records of your personal details, the books you've borrowed, your reading habits – all this information is private and held by the library, and you trust they won't share that information with other people.

This information is centralized in these institutions with each of them maintaining their own records and systems.

The common theme from everyday transactions is that we trust the institutions and the centralized databases they maintain to accurately keep a record of our lives.

Another common underlying theme is that we don't trust each other.

Try to imagine the above scenarios without the trusted centralized organization involved in the transactions.

Imagine you own a shop and someone hands you a piece of paper that has written on it "I owe you $100" with their name signed on it. They tell you that if you take that piece of paper to another shop, you can use it to buy $100 worth of goods from that shop.

Would you trust them?

The answer is probably not, yet that is exactly what people do every day with paper currency. A $100 note is just a piece of paper with an "I owe you $100" from the government on it. You accept and use these notes almost every day trusting that shops will accept them, and they trust that other sellers will accept them and so on.

Where the blockchain offers significant potential is within countries where people don't trust banks, institutions, governments, currencies or each other.

Even in the United States, which has one of the most developed and regulated financial systems in the world, major financial institutions failed during the Great Financial Crisis. Financial companies that had existed for hundreds of years collapsed almost overnight taking people's life savings with them.

In 2015 in Greece, a developed country that is part of the Euro, banks froze all bank account deposits and only allowed people to withdraw around $70 a day from ATMs.

What alternative did people have other than deposit money in what they believed were trustworthy banks and companies? Keep all their cash and hide it under a mattress? If someone finds out your life savings are in your house, then you risk them stealing it. If your house catches on fire, then you risk losing all your money in a fire.

If banks can collapse and governments can freeze bank withdrawals in the USA and Europe, how can people in less developed and regulated countries trust their banks and governments?

The simple answer is they can't trust them.

Trust issues and the blockchain

There are billions of people in the world living in countries where the governments are run by military dictatorships, the governments own the banks and steal or seize money from accounts, the local currency is not accepted at shops, crime is high, and there are no legal systems to protect people and their assets.

There are many countries where even if you can trust the banks won't steal your money or collapse, your deposits are monitored carefully by the government and they could arrest, imprison or execute you based on your transactions.

In the example of a library, a seemingly harmless centralized database for you to share information with. You may borrow a book from the library that the government in that country disapproves of such as Beginners guide to overthrowing a military dictatorship or George Orwell's 1984. The government may flag your reading habits as suspicious potentially leading to an investigation of your personal life, arrest or worse in certain countries.

In countries where there is a lack of trust in companies and governments, it makes transactions risky and difficult. If people put money in a bank, they risk the bank or government stealing it. When making a large purchase like buying a house, people may be forced to keep the money in cash, gold, gems or metals to save up for this large purchase taking on risks that this money is stolen or destroyed in a fire.

Even after all this risk, if someone can save enough money for a large purchase such as a house, they still risk the seller of that house stealing their money and not providing them the ownership of the house. There is no stable legal system to challenge the ownership or report the theft. If the purchase was paid in cash or gold and not an electronic transaction, there is also no evidence the transaction occurred.

Centralized databases and institutions work when there is trust in the system of law, regulations, government, finance, and people. Even when all these factors can be trusted in a country, this trust is still sometimes betrayed causing people to lose money and assets.

A decentralized database built on the blockchain removes the need for centralized institutions and databases. Everyone on the blockchain can view and validate transactions creating transparency and trust.

Trust lays at the core of the blockchain; it provides a system of trust between people without the need for an intermediary involved in the transactions.

The blockchain allows people to transact between each other with anything of value. In the example provided it was books, but this can be used for property, shares, money, digital files... almost anything.

Difference between blockchain and Bitcoin

The first reference to blockchain was within the source code of Bitcoin—essentially the first blockchain was created when Bitcoin was created. The history of Bitcoin and blockchain will be covered in the next chapter, so this chapter won't go over this in detail.

Blockchain is one of the underlying technologies of Bitcoin. There is a misunderstanding that the blockchain is the only technology behind Bitcoin. However, Bitcoin has been created using a range of other cryptographic technologies combined with the blockchain.

Bitcoin is a digital currency, primarily used for payments. Bitcoin uses a one-way blockchain technology; however, the blockchain can be used to record and transfer anything of value, not just financial transactions.

Blockchain-based systems are being used for a wide range of applications across different industries, including digital identities, social networks, voting, cloud storage, decentralized applications and more covered later in the book. There are seemingly endless possibilities for blockchain-based systems that companies and governments are currently developing.

Bitcoin, on the other hand, is still only being used for digital payments. While Bitcoin is gaining in popularity with its price continually hitting record highs, it is designed primarily as a method of payment.

In the next chapter, we'll go into detail with examples of how exactly the blockchain works.

Key points:

- The blockchain is like a database; it is a way of storing records of value and transactions. Almost anything can be recorded on the blockchain.

- Most transactions today between people require an intermediary to provide trust, security, and facilitate the transaction, e.g., banks, financial institutions.

- Blockchain technology removes the need for an intermediary, allowing people to transact directly with each other.

- Billions of people in the world live in countries where they can't trust intermediaries such as banks, governments, and legal systems for transactions or accurate record keeping. Blockchains are particularly useful in these cases to help provide trust and assurance to people when transacting with each other.

- Bitcoin is a blockchain-based system. The blockchain is not a Bitcoin-based system.

- Bitcoin is mainly used for payments. Blockchain-based systems have a wide range of uses to transfer almost anything of value.

Chapter Two: How the Blockchain Works

Note: This chapter is a general, non-technical guide to how the blockchain works.

For a more technical guide on how the blockchain works, see chapter ten towards the end of the book titled, "Technical Guide to the Blockchain."

The previous chapter introduced you to blockchain technology with a brief overview of how it can be used to replace intermediaries in transactions. In this chapter, we'll go into detail with examples of how the blockchain works.

If we go back to the example of a library from the previous chapter, a library is an intermediary that maintains a centralized database of people borrowing books.

If someone has borrowed a book that you want to borrow, you can request the library notify you when that book is returned, but the library won't tell you the details of the person that borrowed that book.

The person that has that book may live on your street, closer than the library is for both of you, but you can't go to their house and ask them if you can borrow it from them. The library maintains the central database of all that information of books borrowed and doesn't share it with the members.

Now, imagine a shared library where you contribute your books and allow people to borrow them from you. You probably have lots of books that other people would want to borrow from you, and there are likely many other people that have books you would want to borrow and read.

In this example of a shared library, anybody can join, and when they borrow books, they can also lend the books to other people, without bringing it back to the library or original owner.

How would you maintain those records of who had borrowed books, which book they had, and who the original owner of the book was?

The records you need to maintain are not just for your books, but for everyone's books in the shared library. You need to maintain a record of everyone's books currently in the library, the original owners, the books that have been borrowed, along with whom other people have lent the books to.

You could assign one person in the group to maintain the records, but you are just back to having the original library and centralized database model.

This may seem complicated, and at this point, you may be asking yourself why did I agree to join this shared library when I can just get these books on Kindle.

This is a situation where the benefits of blockchain technology can really be seen over traditional databases.

The blockchain can provide a decentralized distributed database of all the records of the books in the library.

With a decentralized database, everyone in the library gets access to the records. They would see all the books in the library, who the original owners were, who has borrowed each book, they could see if they went on to lend that book to someone else.

Every time a book is borrowed from the shared library, all the database records of books that everybody has access to are updated. There is no central database or institution required to operate this; everybody maintains the database.

You can operate a library without the need for a central database and external institution operating it.

Why is it called blockchain?

In the library example, every time a book is borrowed it creates a transaction. There are lots of transactions occurring at the same time, so these transactions are then grouped together and added to a new block.

This new block is added "on top" of the previous block by referring to the block before it, linking them together.

For example:

Block 10 links to block 9
Block 9 links to block 8
Block 8 links to block 7
Etc.

By linking these blocks together, it creates a chain of blocks, hence the name "blockchain." Each new block refers to the previous block, and that block refers to the block before it all the way back to the start.

In the library example, anybody could go to the newest block on the chain. They could see all the books that have been borrowed and by whom. They could then see the transactions in the previous block, to see who had the books before them, all the way back to the start to see the original owner.

There is no central database or authority; if a person wants to claim they are the original owner of the book, it can be traced from the latest block of transactions all the way to the first block known as the "genesis block."

Changing transactions and blocks after they've been added

Blocks added to the blockchain can't be tampered with or changed, they are permanently added to the blockchain. As each block refers to the previous block, if someone wants to commit fraud by changing a transaction, they will have to change all the blocks before and after that block.

The Bitcoin network estimates that after 6 blocks are added on top of a block, it is impossible to change any transactions in that block as the computing power required would make it unfeasible to change.

If a transaction occurs in block number 10, then once the blockchain reaches block 16, it will be impossible to change transactions in block 10.

The number of blocks on top of a transaction can also be referred to as confirmations; some companies will wait for 6 confirmations before accepting a payment as assurance the transaction won't be changed on the blockchain.

Double spending

To understand another problem that blockchain solves, let's look at this example where someone wants to profit from the shared library system by stealing books.

Every time a book is borrowed, it creates a pending transaction, this transaction is sent to everyone on the network to validate and add to the blockchain. The person that groups it with other pending transactions and adds a valid block of transactions to the blockchain gets a reward.

The new block of transactions is added to the blockchain and everyone's database is updated with a record of transactions.

Everyone in the network can see who has each book and the person they borrowed them from. As everybody knows who has each book, the entire network can see if anyone doesn't return a book and the status at any time.

Exchange of value on the blockchain

Let's add another factor to this shared library, every time someone borrows a book, they pay the person they borrowed the book from a token called "bookcoin."

Assuming a person can only lend the books to other people to make a profit, they would have paid 1 bookcoin to borrow the book and would have received 1 bookcoin when someone borrows the book from them. To make a profit, they would need to be lending out more books than they borrow.

Sneaky Sam has joined this shared library. He has joined despite the other members suspecting he would do something sneaky.

Anyway, Sneaky Sam contributes the book Romeo and Juliet to the library, someone borrows the book from the library, and he gets 1 bookcoin

Being the sneaky person that he is, he comes up with a plan to try and borrow more books than he can afford from his bookcoin balance.

Sneaky Sam borrows the book 1984 from David.
Sneaky Sam then quickly goes borrows the book Hamlet from Sally.

Both create transactions on the network. The first transaction is sent to everyone on the network to approve the lending of the book "1984" and that Sneaky Sam pays David 1 bookcoin for borrowing this book.

This transaction is decided by everyone on the network is valid and they add to a new block, which is added to the blockchain:
Sneaky Sam borrows 1984 from David
Sneaky Sam pays 1 bookcoin to David.

After this transaction goes through, the network receives the next transaction to approve:
Sneaky Sam borrows Hamlet from Sally
Sneaky Sam pays 1 bookcoin to Sally.

The network checks Sneaky Sam's book balance and sees that he only had 1 bookcoin, and he is trying to create copies of the coins to try and trick the network.

As the network is open and everyone has a copy of the records, they can trace the transactions all the way to the beginning. They can see where Sneaky Sam received 1 bookcoin from lending his book giving him a balance of 1 bookcoin.

He doesn't have 2 bookcoins to spend and everyone on the network can see that. The majority of people on the network agree this is an invalid transaction. They don't allow him to borrow a second book and this payment is considered invalid. The transaction is rejected and not added to the blockchain.

Distributed consensus

In this example, it was mentioned that the majority of people on the network need to agree that a transaction is valid for it to take place, this is known as distributed consensus.

It would not be viable for everyone on the network to agree as there would be people on the network trying to enter double transactions, cheat the system by trying to approve fake transactions as valid.

With many blockchains the threshold of consensus is over 50%, if more than 50% of people on the network agree that a transaction is valid then it is accepted as valid.

This is how decentralized blockchains generally work for approving transactions and managing the network. Instead of one entity approving all the transactions and keeping the database accurate, this is shared among the network. All people connected to the network are able to have a say in whether a transaction should be accepted to the blockchain or not.

The potential risk and dangers of more than 50% of the network accepting an invalid transaction will be discussed later in the book.

Mining

You may have heard the word "mining" used when talking about Bitcoin and cryptocurrencies.

Transaction requests are sent to every computer on the network to validate and include them in the blockchain.

In order to validate a transaction and add it to the blockchain, the computers on the network must solve a puzzle connected to the next block to be added to the blockchain.

The computer that correctly solves the puzzle first, can add the transactions into a block, then add that block of transactions to the blockchain.

For solving the puzzle first, they receive a reward, usually paid in the cryptocurrency or token used on that network.

This process is known as mining, as it is like mining small amounts of value out of a block.

Proof of work

Miners that solve the puzzles and add valid blocks to the network are rewarded for contributing computer power, electricity, and resources to the network as this helps keep the network running.

The puzzle they solve is known as proof of work. It is a mathematical puzzle that is very difficult to solve but easy to verify the answer once it has been solved.

Think of it as a combination lock. In order to add a new block to the blockchain and receive a reward, you must solve the combination to the lock.

You can only solve the combination to this lock by guessing the numbers. Everyone on the network randomly guesses the number to this combination lock. The person that solves it first gets a reward and can add a block to the blockchain.

Once the combination of the lock is solved, everyone else on the network can easily put those numbers into the lock to confirm that the numbers open the lock.

By solving this puzzle, it acts as proof that computing power, electricity, time and resources were contributed to the network. The reward is compensation for the cost of contributing these resources to running the blockchain.

Proof of work takes a lot of computing power and there are other methods that can be used when running a blockchain that will be discussed later.

Summary of how the blockchain works
We've covered how a blockchain network could be used to create a database to replace a library as a centralized institution.

For many, the usefulness of replacing a library database may not be as important today when almost everything is digital. However, the books can be replaced by almost anything of value.

If we replace the books with ownership of property titles in the example, we can see that ownership of a property can be transferred and managed via blockchain.

When ownership of a property is transferred, everyone on the network receives notification about the transfer of property, the majority on the network approves the transfer of ownership, and it is added to the blockchain as a record that everyone can see.

If the owner of the property tries to sell their property title to 2 different people, everyone on the network will see the duplicate transfer and one of the transfers will be rejected by the network.

As mentioned in the previous chapter, where blockchain networks could have the most potential are countries where companies, banks institutions, and governments can't be trusted and record keeping is manual or unreliable. Being able to replace centralized databases and institutions with a blockchain network for property records could have huge benefits for people in these countries.

We've mainly looked at how blockchain technology works on a general level and covered a few examples of where it could be used. Later in the book, we'll cover more examples of areas where blockchain networks could replace existing technology and institutions.

Key Points:

- In order for a transaction to be processed and considered valid, it is grouped with other transactions and added to a new block.

- This new block is added "on top" of the previous block in the blockchain. Each block refers to the previous block number, linking them together like a chain, which is where the name "blockchain" comes from.

- The chain of blocks in the blockchain links all the way back to the first block on the chain known as the "genesis block."

- With a decentralized blockchain, each block of transactions on the blockchain is validated by the network. Everybody on the network receives information about transactions on the network; it is not controlled by a centralized database owned by one company or institution.

- Once a block of transactions has been added to the blockchain, it is difficult to reverse. Every block added on top is a confirmation that the transaction won't be reversed. The more blocks on top, the harder it is to reverse until it is unfeasible. On the Bitcoin network, 6 blocks are accepted as confirmation the transaction won't be reversed.

- With distributed consensus, the majority of computers on the network need to agree that a transaction is valid before it is accepted on the blockchain.

- Double spending is where someone on the network attempts to duplicate transactions. This is generally done by sending transactions more than once before one of them is confirmed and accepted onto the blockchain.

- A double spending attack is where a user controls more than 50% of the computers on the network. This allows the user to double spend transactions by controlling which transactions are accepted and rejected.

- Mining is the process of validating transactions and adding new blocks to the blockchain. Small rewards are given for each new block added to the blockchain, like mining a small reward out of a big block.

- Proof of work involves solving a computer puzzle to add a new block to the blockchain. It is difficult to solve but easy to prove, like a combination lock. It provides evidence that computing power and resources were used and contributed to the network.

Chapter Three: History of the Blockchain And Bitcoin

"I think the fact that within the bitcoin universe an algorithm replaces the functions of [the government] … is actually pretty cool. I am a big fan of Bitcoin."

--Al Gore, 45th Vice President of the United States

The blockchain was first mentioned in the original code for Bitcoin. While there is now a separation between blockchain technology and Bitcoin, the history of blockchain is linked to the history of Bitcoin, so this chapter will cover the interlinked history.

Cryptography is a key underlying foundation of the blockchain. Cryptography has a long history of protecting secrets and messages that dates back thousands of years. A famous example of ancient cryptography was the "Caesar Cipher" used by Julius Caesar when he sent written communication containing sensitive information.

The Caesar Cipher involved replacing each letter in the message with a different letter of the alphabet a set number of letters away. For example, all letters may be moved 3 letters forward, A would become D, B would become E, C would become F and so on until every letter in the message was replaced. Only the person that knew the number each letter had been moved would be able to read the message easily.

Literacy levels were low at the time and there were many different languages spoken around the world, so enemies intercepting messages would be unable to read them or assume the letters were written in a foreign language. This was a simple method that is easily deciphered today; however, at the time it was effective enough to make communications difficult to intercept.

Modern cryptography has come a long way from its origins, but the basic foundations are similar. Messages or data are covered up by replacing the letters and numbers so the original message can't be read unless the person has the secret code or method to decrypt it.

Skipping forward to the cryptography underlying blockchain technology, several papers were published between the 80s and 90s proposing data could be secured through cryptography while linking that data securely in chains along with proposals for digital currencies.

In 1982, David Chaum wrote a paper titled "Blind Signatures For Untraceable Payments." Due to this paper, David Chaum is credited as being the inventor of digital cash and blind signatures. Blind signatures hide the content of a message before it is signed, the digital signature can be verified against the original while the contents remain hidden, which is an early version of the cryptographic signatures used by cryptocurrencies.

This and subsequent papers that David Chaum published proposed that users could obtain and spend digital currency in a way that was untraceable by banks or other institutions. David Chaum along with Amos Fiat and Moni Naor also proposed offline transactions that would be able to detect if the cash had previously been spent, a possible solution to the issue of double-spending.

In 1990, David founded DigiCash to create a digital currency based on the ideas in his papers. Then in 1994, the first DigiCash electronic payment was sent. The start of the DigiCash press release of 1994 is below:

```
"World's first electronic cash payment over
computer networks. (Release Date: May 27,
1994)

Electronic cash has the privacy of paper cash,
while achieving the high security required for
electronic network environments exclusively
through innovations in public key
cryptography."
```

This press release was 14 years ahead of the creation of Bitcoin, and yet if you replace the words "electronic cash" with "Bitcoin" in the press release, it could be issued as a press release for Bitcoin today.

DigiCash created the first electronic cash system that was untraceable by banks, governments or other institutions. It used cryptography, private and public keys and signatures for hiding content of messages in much the same way cryptocurrencies do today.

DigiCash was perhaps too far ahead of its time as most people had not even heard of the internet in 1994. DigiCash declared bankruptcy in 1998 and its assets were sold to eCash technologies, which was another company focused on digital currencies.

In the early days of the internet, email spam was becoming a problem that nobody had created a solution for yet. In 1997, Adam Back proposed a system to limit email spam along with denial-of-service attacks by using a proof-of-work algorithm known as hashcash.

This proof-of-work algorithm required that the system sending an email solves a computer puzzle, then place the answer in the header of the email. This required the sender to use computing power and resources to send emails, making it more difficult to send bulk spam emails. This puzzle is difficult to solve for the sender but easy to verify the answer is correct for the receiver of the email, filtering spam emails that didn't complete this proof-of-work.

In 1998, Nick Szabo proposed a decentralized digital currency called "bit gold." In the proposal for bit gold, people would allocate computing resources to solving cryptographic puzzles. The majority of the network would have to accept the answer as valid before moving on to the next puzzle. Once a puzzle was solved and accepted by the network, it would become part of the next puzzle to be solved by the network. The puzzles were time stamped and as each answer became part of the next puzzle they were linked together like a chain.

At the time, Nick Szabo stated that digital currencies face the issue of double spending as they can just be copied and pasted unless control is given to a central bank or authority. His work on bit gold was an attempt to solve this double-spending problem combined with a decentralized digital currency.

Bit gold was never created as a real currency; it only existed in theory. However, it is considered as having laid the groundwork that the later Bitcoin and blockchain technology was built on.

In 1998, Wei Dai published another paper titled "B-Money, An Anonymous, Distributed Electronic Cash System." The paper outlined the foundations for cryptocurrencies, including Bitcoin, and the paper is referenced in Satoshi Nakamoto's Bitcoin paper.

In the paper by Wei Dai, it states that an electronic cash system required the below to function:
- An amount of computational work and proof of that work.
- Rewards allocated for the computational work completed.
- A collective group ledger that is verified and updated by all members.
- Transfers of fund completed on the collective group ledgers and verified with cryptographic hashes.
- All transactions are signed with digital signatures using public key cryptography and verified by the network.

In 2000, Stefan Konst published a paper that provided practical solutions for implementing cryptographically secured chains.

It was the work between the 1980s to 2000s, along with the academic papers published, that laid the groundwork for Bitcoin and the blockchain.

In 2008, Satoshi Nakamoto (which is widely regarded as a pseudonym) posted a paper on the internet entitled "Bitcoin: A Peer-to-Peer Electronic Cash System." This paper outlines the creation of Bitcoin and blocks of transactions linked in chains. The paper never directly uses the words "block chain" together when referring to this method.

In 2009, Bitcoin became more than just an idea in an academic paper when Satoshi Nakamoto created the Bitcoin network along with the first blockchain. The first mention of blockchain was as separate words "block chain," in the original source code for Bitcoin.

This first blockchain was a core feature of Bitcoin, preventing double spending and acting as a distributed public ledger for all transactions on the Bitcoin network.

Nakamoto is credited with the mining of the first block on the Bitcoin network known as the "genesis block."

In the "Genesis Block," Satoshi Nakamoto left the message: "The Times 03/Jan/2009 Chancellor on brink of second bailout for banks"

This message may have been left as proof that the date the block was created was on or after the 3rd of January, along with being a comment about the failures within the current structure of banking and currency markets. As this headline is from a newspaper in the United Kingdom, it's possible that Satoshi was living in the U.K at the time.

The words "block" and "chain" were used separately with Bitcoin and even when it gained mainstream awareness. It was not until years later that it became one word: blockchain.

The original Bitcoin blockchain was not without error. Like most major technology and business ventures there were problems along the way. During August 2010, the first major issue with Bitcoin protocols was discovered. Transactions were found that had been altered before they were recorded in the blockchain, tampering with the official transactions. Somehow people were bypassing Bitcoin's inbuilt restrictions and creating an infinite number by altering original transactions up and then skimming off the top.

The vulnerability within the system was exploited and over 184 billion bitcoins were generated from a single transaction and sent to only two addresses on the network. Within hours the transaction had been spotted, and subsequently erased, from the blockchain. The Bitcoin network went through an updated overhaul, and to this day an issue like that has not occurred since.

In 2011, the drug marketplace "Silk Road" was launched. It was a marketplace site like eBay that enabled people to buy and sell drugs online. Bitcoin was the main form of payment on Silk Road, and while this led to an increase in the use of Bitcoin, it also associated Bitcoin with drug dealing and illegal activities.

Bitcoin continued to gain popularity and public awareness. In 2013, Bitcoin reached a peak of around $1,000 USD, and despite criticism from law enforcement and governments, it seemed unstoppable.

Then in 2013, Silk Road was shut down by the FBI with all assets seized and the creator arrested facing life in prison. Around the same time, the largest Bitcoin exchange Mt. Gox, which was handling 70% of all Bitcoin transactions, received warrants, fines, and faced regulation issues from various US government departments. By the end of 2013, Mt. Gox had suspended withdrawals into US Dollars and declared bankruptcy in early 2014.

Other cryptocurrencies had started to pop up based on the Bitcoin source code using different blockchains. Litecoin was split from the original Bitcoin blockchain as a fork in the blockchain; it became a separate cryptocurrency and blockchain with a lower tlme to add blocks to the blockchain along with other changes. A block is added to the Bitcoin blockchain around every 10 minutes, Litecoin adds a block to the blockchain every 2 and a half minutes.

After Mt. Gox and Silk Road were shut down, Bitcoin fell from a peak of $1,000 down to around $200. New cryptocurrencies were created and many people publicly declared that Bitcoin was finished.

However, Bitcoin was far from over. In fact, with Silk Road shut down, Bitcoin began to be less associated with drug dealing and crime and companies started to pay interest to the technology behind Bitcoin.

It was still difficult to get large companies, banks, and financial firms to take Bitcoin seriously as it was hard to forget the failure of Mt. Gox, drug dealing, and hitmen paid with Bitcoin. Even without the crime associated with it, many people still considered Bitcoin to be fake internet money, a fad, a financial currency bubble or a scam.

The word Bitcoin still had many negative connotations around it, but the word "blockchain" was a respectable word to use when discussing the technology. Using the word blockchain separated the technology from the Bitcoin internet currency or Bitcoin network. Investors and financial institutions weren't interested in Bitcoin, but they started to become very interested in blockchain technology.

The price of Bitcoin, along with the levels of interest in Bitcoin was low in 2014. However, the interest in blockchain was gaining momentum. Blockchain was starting to be used with reference to distributed ledgers and databases instead of currencies. People were proposing that outdated, manual ledgers for recording data entries could be replaced with blockchains.

In 2015, the live blockchain of Ethereum was launched. This launch took the possibilities of blockchain technology to another level. The Ethereum network allows decentralized applications to run on a blockchain along with smart contracts. Smart contracts and decentralized apps are seen by many as the future direction of blockchain technology, often referred to as Blockchain 2.0.

Most major banks and financial service companies around the world are developing blockchain-based systems to replace existing databases or networks. With the ease of access, along with the functionality that decentralized apps combined with smart contracts provide it has opened blockchain technology to almost every industry. Programmers at home are able to build software that runs on a blockchain without the need to create their own blockchain.

In 2017, Harvard Business Review declared that blockchain could potentially create new foundations in economic and social systems. This statement appears to be how blockchain developing is unfolding; it is reminiscent of the internet in its infancy with untold potential that is just being realized. Large companies, start-ups, venture capitalists, governments, and programmers are all working on blockchain-based systems, databases, and decentralized applications.

By now you should have an understanding of what the blockchain is and the history of its development. In the next chapters, we'll cover the benefits, disadvantages, danger, and the potential future of blockchain technology.

Key Points:

- Cryptography is the underlying foundation of the blockchain. Cryptography dates back thousands of years when messages were written in codes to protect them from enemies.

- Several papers were published during the 80s and 90s theorizing the use of cryptography combined with secure data chains and creation of digital currencies.

- 1982 – David Chaum wrote a paper titled "Blind Signatures For Untraceable Payments." David Chaum is credited as being the inventor of digital cash and blind signatures.

- 1990 – David founded DigiCash which created an untraceable digital currency using cryptography, private and public keys and signatures. DigiCash declared bankruptcy in 1998 and its assets were sold to eCash technologies.

- 1997 – Adam Back created a proof-of-work algorithm to limit email spam known as hashcash. It required the sender of an email to prove they solved a computer puzzle before sending an email. This used computing power and resources, making it more expensive to send bulk spam emails.

- 1998 – Nick Szabo proposed a decentralized digital currency called "bit gold." This incorporated proof-of-work combined with a network of computers that accepted the proof-of-work as valid and incorporated it into the next puzzle with a timestamp. Bit gold was never created as a real currency; it only existed in theory.

- 1998 – Wei Dai published another paper titled, "B-Money, An Anonymous, Distributed Electronic Cash System." The paper outlined the foundations for cryptocurrencies, including Bitcoin, and the paper is referenced in Satoshi Nakamoto's Bitcoin paper.

- It was the work during the 1980s to 2000s, along with the academic papers published, that laid the groundwork for Bitcoin and the blockchain.

- 2008 – Satoshi Nakamoto (which is widely regarded as a pseudonym) posted a paper on the internet entitled "Bitcoin: A Peer-to-Peer Electronic Cash System." This paper outlines the creation of Bitcoin and blocks of transactions linked in chains. The paper never directly uses the words "block chain" together when referring to this method.

- 2009 – Bitcoin became more than just an idea in an academic paper when Satoshi Nakamoto created the Bitcoin network along with the first blockchain. The first mention of blockchain was as separate words "block chain," in the original source code for Bitcoin.

- This first blockchain was a core feature of Bitcoin, preventing double spending and acting as a distributed public ledger for all transactions on the Bitcoin network.

- Nakamoto is credited with the mining of the first block on the Bitcoin network known as the "genesis block" with the message in it:
  "The Times 03/Jan/2009 Chancellor on brink of second bailout for banks."

  This message may have been left as proof that the date the first block was created was on or after the 3rd of January, along with being a comment about the failures within the current structure of banking and currency markets.

- The creator of Bitcoin and the blockchain, Satoshi Nakamoto, is still unknown. People suspect Nick Szabo or Wei Dei of being the creators of Bitcoin; however, they both deny it.

- 2015 – Ethereum blockchain launched, allowing decentralized applications and smart contacts to run on the blockchain. This enhanced functionality of blockchain technology is known as Blockchain 2.0.

Chapter Four: Benefits of Blockchain technology

"Blockchain technology has the ability to optimize the global infrastructure to deal with global issues in this space much more efficiently than current systems."
– Marwan Forzley, Founder of Align Commerce

In the first few chapters, we've covered what the blockchain is, how it works and some examples of potential uses. Some of the benefits were briefly mentioned in the previous chapters, but in this chapter, we'll go into more detail about the benefits of blockchain technology.

Transparency

Blockchain-based systems offer improvements in transparency compared to existing record-keeping and ledgers. Changes to the ledger are visible to everyone on the network, and the transactions can't be altered or deleted once entered onto the blockchain.

With existing record-keeping, a person could go and alter the database and hide the change from people. There have been countless examples where massive cases of fraud went undetected as the ledgers were not transparent. This lack of transparency allowed people to alter entries or manipulate data without other people knowing about the changes.

Blockchain-based technology provides transparency to all people on the network, with transactions visible to all connected computers. The majority of computers connected to the blockchain must approve transactions or changes to the blockchain preventing transactions from being hidden or manipulated.

All changes are in near real-time; this process occurs as transactions are approved and added to the blockchain. This scenario of a person in an organization stealing money or hiding company losses by manipulating entries in ledgers is much less likely to occur on a blockchain-based distributed ledger.

Moving to a blockchain in different industries provides transparency across a range of areas. With a financial transaction, you can watch the status of the transfer on the blockchain in real time, instead of not knowing the status of a transaction until it is completed, which is often the case with today's systems.

This same transparency applies to anything of value that is recorded on the blockchain. In later chapters, we'll look at different industries that blockchain technology is being developed and the transparency this provides to customers and businesses compared to existing systems.

Removal of intermediaries

As discussed at the start of the book, most transactions today between people require intermediaries such as banks to provide trust and security for transactions.

An advantage of Blockchain technology over existing systems is the ability to remove intermediaries allowing transactions to occur directly between people instead of involving a third party.
This greatly benefits billions of people in the world that live in countries where they can't trust third-party intermediaries due to corrupt governments, high crime rates, poor regulation of companies, manual record keeping or limited legal options to pursue claims.
Blockchains are particularly useful in these cases where the trust in the intermediaries doesn't exist and transacting directly with people is difficult or risky as well.

The blockchain provides trust and transparency while reducing the risks involved in transactions, without the need of a third party to act as an intermediary in transactions.

Decentralization

The decentralization of a blockchain database is a key component of how intermediaries can be removed while at the same time increasing transparency and trust. Blockchains are maintained on a single shared ledger, instead of multiple ledgers that are privately managed by different institutions. People and companies do not have to give up control to a single institution when using a blockchain. This makes collaboration between parties faster and easier to manage.

To use the example of a group of banks transferring assets between each other, in the current structures and systems each bank would maintain their own ledgers and transaction records separately. By using a blockchain-based ledger, they would only need to reconcile transactions to one shared ledger that all banks would have access to and agree on the correct record of transactions.

The decentralized structure of the blockchain is an advantage to companies that may be competitors but are working together as part of an industry group or consortium. A company may be wary about handing over data or collaborating on a database that is owned by a competitor. Competitors working together, where one party owns all the data could involve lengthy legal contracts and non-disclosure agreements protecting the privacy and access of the data. However, with a blockchain-based system, competitors can work together on a shared database they all have full access and control over.

Centralized databases are prone to hacking, data loss, and corruption. The blockchain has no central database that is a point of failure, manipulation or corruption of data. All computers on the blockchain network have a copy of the blockchain, reducing the risk of data loss. To manipulate the data on a blockchain requires "hacking" over 50% of the computers on the network at the same time, which is almost completely unfeasible.

Trust

As mentioned previously in the book, current methods for transacting between people requires trust in an intermediary to facilitate the process.

The blockchain allows intermediaries to be removed while still maintaining trust and security between the people involved in the transaction.

The trust is placed in the blockchain network instead of a third party. Blockchain networks are generally decentralized, with all people connected to the network having access to the blockchain.

The removal of intermediaries, improved transparency and decentralized structure of the blockchain have already been covered above. It is the increase in trust between entities in a transaction that is an important non-tangible benefit of these changes.

Security

Data entered onto a blockchain is immutable, meaning it can't be altered or changed. Every block of data on the blockchain can also be traced back to the first "genesis block."

The immutability of data entered combined blocks connected all the way back to the first block on the blockchain, creates an easy to follow audit trail of every transaction on the blockchain.

Throughout history there have been countless cases of fraud and manipulation of data. Often when fraud is committed, the trail leading to the occurrence of fraud is altered making it difficult and time-consuming to investigate. The trail of data may have been altered so much that it's impossible to trace the transactions and fraud.

With a blockchain-based system, past transactions can't be altered leaving a clear trail of what has occurred on the blockchain. As mentioned in the decentralized section of the blockchain, altering an existing transaction would require controlling over 50% of the computers on the network at the same time, which is almost completely unfeasible. If this did occur, it would also be quickly spotted by the other computers connected to the network anyway.

The security of the blockchain is not flawless, but currently existing systems have proven to be far from secure time and time again. While fraud may never be fully eliminated, the blockchain provides a clear audit trail back to the start allowing attempts at fraud to be easily identified. This solves many of the security issues in conventional systems.

Wide range of potential uses

Almost anything of value can be recorded on the blockchain, the phrase "anything of value," doesn't necessarily mean financial value. In the first chapter, the example provided it was books, but this could be a record of ownership, a digital identity, copyright license, digital files or anything that could currently be recorded in a database

With the example of copyright licenses, these are assets of value however the licenses are just data or numbers stored in a database. The value comes from these licenses protecting the ownership and income derived from what the copyright protects.

There are organizations and associations that control and manage copyright licenses in a centralized database. These licenses are assets of value that can be stored on the blockchain removing the need for the organizations that control the licenses. Assets of value such as cryptocurrencies, licenses and other digital assets can exist solely on the blockchain as native blockchain assets making them easier to manage than existing records of ownership.

Blockchain technology is an easily accessible new technology, especially with recent innovations such as the Ethereum platform and smart contracts. This allows anyone to develop applications that utilize blockchain technology.

Blockchain has the potential to change almost every industry in the world. The projects being developed show the impact blockchain technology could have on everyday life with many companies already developing their own blockchain systems.

Later in the book, we'll go into more detail about the different industries and uses for blockchain technology with examples of projects currently being developed.

Reduced costs

Blockchain technology could significantly reduce costs in many industries by removing intermediaries involved in the process of recording and transferring assets. Every intermediary or layer involved in a transaction adds costs to recording and transferring assets.

In current systems, when transferring assets or recording them, there are often multiple ledgers and databases that each organization maintains. A distributed ledger allows parties to transfer assets on one shared ledger, reducing the costs of maintaining multiple ledgers in each organization.

Maintaining ledgers or databases is costly and often a very manual process with many people involved in checking the integrity of each ledger. Blockchain-based distributed ledgers reduce the costs by replacing individual ledgers with one shared ledger, providing real-time settlement and auditing from all parties connected to the network each time a transaction occurs.

Increased transaction speed

Blockchain-based systems not only reduce the costs involved in transactions but they dramatically increase the speed as well. By removing intermediaries and settling transactions on a shared distributed ledger, blockchain-based ledgers can settle transactions almost instantly.

If you've transferred money from a bank account, you may have noticed the funds were removed from your account; however, they were not received in the other account until days later.

Likewise, with credit card purchases, transactions may show as pending for several days on a credit card statement. For store owners, they provide goods to the buyer but do not receive the payment for days later when the credit card company settles the transaction.

In these examples above, blockchain-based systems are being developed to increase the speed of these transactions. However, it isn't limited to just these examples, any type of transaction or transfer of value could potentially use blockchain technology to increase the speed of transactions.

Later in the book, we'll cover real-world examples of companies that are developing a blockchain-based system to increase the speed of transactions in finance and other industries.

Final note

Most of the information published about blockchain technology relates to the benefits, advantages, and hype around its potential. While this chapter has covered a lot of benefits to using blockchain-based systems, that doesn't mean it's flawless or the answer to all the problems within an industry.

In the next chapter, we'll cover some of the disadvantages and dangers of using blockchain-based systems.

Key Points:

Transparency – Blockchain offers significant improvements in transparency compared to existing record-keeping and ledgers for many industries.

Removal of Intermediaries – Blockchain-based systems allow for the removal of intermediaries involved in the record keeping and transfer of assets.

Decentralization – Blockchain-based systems can run on a decentralized network of computers, reducing the risk of hacking, server downtime and loss of data.

Trust – Blockchain-based systems increase trust between parties involved in a transaction through improved transparency and decentralized networks along with the removal of third-party intermediaries in countries where trust in the intermediaries doesn't exist.

Security – Data entered on the blockchain is immutable, preventing against fraud through manipulating transactions and the history of data. Transactions entered on the blockchain provide a clear trail to the very start of the blockchain allowing any transaction to be easily investigated and audited.

Wide range of uses – Almost anything of value can be recorded on the blockchain, and there are many companies and industries already developing blockchain-based systems. These examples are covered later in the book.

Easily accessible technology – Along with the wide range of uses, blockchain technology makes it easy to create applications without significant investment in infrastructure with recent innovations like the Ethereum platform. Decentralized apps, smart contracts, and the Ethereum platform are covered later in the book.

Reduced costs – Blockchain-based ledgers allow for removal of intermediaries and layers of confirmation involved in transactions. Transactions that may take multiple individual ledgers could be settled on one shared ledger, reducing the costs of validating, confirming and auditing each transaction across multiple organizations.

Increased transaction speed – The removal of intermediaries and settlement on distributed ledgers, allows for dramatically increased transaction speeds compared to a wide range of existing systems.

Disadvantages – There is a wide range of compelling reasons to change from existing systems to blockchain-based systems. However, there are also downsides and risks that should not be ignored.

Chapter Five: Disadvantages / Dangers of Using Blockchain technology

Blockchain was designed specifically for one main goal: preventing the "double spend" of electronic coins, without a central authority. Yet few of the mooted use cases are vulnerable to double spend or anything analogous. At the same time, many important security objectives are not provided by blockchain at all.

Thus, blockchain is neither necessary nor sufficient for many of its suggested applications; in practice it's massively over-engineered, or incomplete, or both.

--Steve Wilson, Beyond the Hype: Understanding the Weak Links in the Blockchain

Blockchain technology is being touted by many as the solution to all the problems in industries and the world at the moment.

There are new blockchain start-ups and cryptocurrencies launched every day promising to do everything from disrupt banking systems to eliminate world poverty.

Many of the claims are reminiscent of the internet in its early days. While the internet did change the world, a lot of the claims were overstated, timeframes were unrealistic, and many start-ups predicted to be successful went bankrupt.

In this chapter, we'll look at some of the issues and disadvantages of blockchain technology.

Lack of Privacy

Decentralized blockchains lack privacy, which will make full acceptance difficult. Not only is the information not private, but it is also readily accessible at any given moment to anyone using the system.

It is relatively easy to figure out the identity of an account on the Bitcoin blockchain after receiving a payment from that person.

If you were to go into a shop and make a payment, the store owner would be able to see that transaction on the blockchain. The information in the transaction would show the wallet that the funds were sent from, they could then check that account and be able to see how much money you own and all your transactions into and out of that account.

The idea that a decentralized blockchain effectively publishes every single transaction they make to public networks is worrying to many people. Especially in the case of in-store purchases where an identity can be directed linked to an account and transactions.

This is also concerning considering that the computers running a large amount of the blockchain networks are in countries such as Russia and China where computer crime is high and personal information may be used against people living or traveling to those countries.

There are decentralized blockchains that provide more privacy with transactions or restrict the people that have access to seeing the information. However, Bitcoin, Ethereum, and many of the largest blockchain cryptocurrencies do not operate this way and currently have no plans to implement further privacy around transactions or accounts.

Security Concerns

Blockchain-based assets are like cash, if the cash in your wallet is stolen or lost, then it's gone. Blockchain-based systems use advanced cryptography and encryption that are more secure than standard internet passwords or number access codes. However, more security can sometimes result in a system being less secure.

There are countless examples with cryptocurrencies where someone has forgotten their private key and can't access their money. You only need to look at forum threads on the internet of people stating warning not to lose your private key along with a story about how they lost their key and now can't access the money in their wallet.

These cases often happen when someone has purchased a particular cryptocurrency at a low price but not paid much attention to it. They later find out the currency has gone up a lot and that initial small investment is worth thousands of dollars now and try to access it again.

Fifty dollars' worth of bitcoin in 2009 would be worth over a million dollars 8 years later, so it's easy to see how this could occur with such large price increases on initially small amounts of money. A well-publicized case of this is James Howells in the U.K, who threw out his laptop containing 7,500 bitcoins on it. At today's price, this is worth over $15 million dollars.

Due to the transparency of the blockchain, if people have their public key they can see their balance and how much it is worth but have no way to access it. This is the equivalent of a bank being able to tell you the balance in your bank account, but you have no way to access it.

With traditional bank accounts, if you lose your password to internet banking, your credit cards or forget your bank account numbers, you can go into a bank and prove your identity to gain access again. This is not the case with decentralized blockchain-based cryptocurrencies like Bitcoin. There have been billions of dollars in cryptocurrencies being stolen through hacking, scams or poor security over the last few years.

If someone were to gain access to your credit card and withdraw funds, you could call the bank and have them cancel your card so the thief couldn't withdraw any more funds. The bank would likely have fraud protection and be able to reverse the transaction and trace the payments.

With blockchain-based systems, transactions can't be altered or reversed, and there is no intermediary to assist you if fraud occurs on your account. If you sent funds to the wrong account number (wallet) on the blockchain, then those funds are gone. If someone gains access to your private key, they can withdraw all the money in your account, and there is no way to reverse that transaction or claim compensation.

The first question on most frequently asked questions pages of blockchain-based systems is "how do I reset my password if I forget it or lose it?" The answer is "you can't." The advice given to people when setting up a private key on the blockchain is to "write it down somewhere." All that advanced cryptography and security results in people writing down private keys and keeping them in their home or on their computer, reducing the security when compared to traditional security methods.

When dealing with mainstream implementation of blockchain-based systems, many of the security methods that make blockchain assets more secure will make mainstream adoption more difficult. Web-based blockchain wallets are popular, where people store cryptocurrencies with a third-party company. When using third-party web-based wallets, people sacrifice the security benefits of the blockchain such as private keys in favor of traditional passwords that can be reset if they forget them anyway.

No Centralized Control

"In financial markets there's always a mechanism to correct an attack. In a blockchain there is no mechanism to correct it — people have to accept it."
- Robert Sams, founder and chief executive of London-based Clearmatics.

Blockchain-based systems are designed to replace third-party intermediaries, putting the responsibility and control back with the individuals involved in transactions.
This control is placed with the majority of people on the network, creating issues with regards to control of the blockchain.

The decentralized nature of many blockchains means that the network must agree and decide the future direction of the network and blockchain. With a traditional network and software, if an organization wants to make a change, they can make that change after approval from with relevant departments within the organization. With a decentralized blockchain network like Bitcoin, changes must be agreed to by a certain majority of the network, this may be over 50% but could be as high as 70% to 80% of the network.

A recent example of this has been the division in the Bitcoin network about implementing either SegWit (Segregated Witness) or Bitcoin Unlimited. Large amounts of the network support different changes for the Bitcoin network and neither side has been able to get the majority required to make the changes.

The disagreement has meant other cryptocurrencies and blockchain networks have been able to move ahead of Bitcoin in terms of technological changes. The disagreement has caused the Bitcoin network to stagnate with slow transaction times, slow confirmation times, and ongoing scalability issues.

Technology such as software constantly changes over time. Decentralized blockchain networks may result in division over the direction of changes, especially where there is a failure to reach a majority agreement. If a majority agreement is reached, there will still be a large number of people on the network that disagree with the changes that have been made.

This makes decentralized networks risky for organizations to use. A company may build a business or software around a network where they have no control over changes that could dramatically impact their software and business.

Risk of 51% attack
Continuing on from the issue of control, if someone were able to control over 50% of the computers on a blockchain network, they would control the transactions on the blockchain. A malicious user controlling over 50% of the computers on a blockchain network is known as a "51% attack."

Leveraging this control over a cryptocurrency network, they would theoretically be able to block new transactions from confirming, reverse transactions, and allow for the dreaded "double-spending" of coins.

A 51% attack on a blockchain network is theoretical as it would be difficult to control such a large amount of the network. However, there are massive mining farms set up in China, Russia, and other parts of the world that control a large part of the computing power of blockchain networks. If these large mining farms collaborated, they could potentially take over blockchain networks and manipulate them to their benefit.

Even without controlling 51% of the network, they can still manipulate the network by allocating their computing power in a way that influences the future development of the network. This has been the case with the division regarding the Bitcoin network mentioned earlier.

Unproven new technology

Blockchain-based systems are an unproven new technology that has mainly been applied to cryptocurrencies. There is a lack of real-world applications that are currently in existence to prove the effectiveness of the technology.

The technology is new with a lot of potential, but most of the potential applications are theoretical. The saying "Build a better mousetrap and the world will beat a path to your door" is a common business fallacy. Just because the technology may be better than existing systems in many ways, it doesn't mean that people will want to use it over existing options.

As mentioned earlier, the cryptographic security is superior to existing security methods; however, if you lose your key to many blockchain-based systems, you can't recover it. People choose to write down their private keys on paper or store it on their computer, so they don't forget it, thus eliminating the benefits of the additional security and potentially making the system less secure.

Another benefit of blockchain networks is removing third-party intermediaries. The process of connecting to blockchain networks, sending transactions, setting up the private keys is complicated and risky for many people. Many people prefer to give access to their private keys to third-party intermediaries with web-wallets or similar software, which eliminates another main benefit of blockchain networks.

Cost

The proof-of-work algorithm that many blockchain networks use requires proof that computing power and resources were contributed to the network before a block is added to the network. This proof is in the form of an answer to a puzzle that is attached to the block for the network to confirm it is correct. Solving this puzzle requires an enormous amount of computing power and electricity.

Professor John Quiggin from the University of Queensland has calculated that every half an hour the Bitcoin network uses the same amount of electricity as the average US household does in an entire year.

The average US household uses 10 to 12,000 kWh in electricity each year, about the same as would be required to generate four Bitcoins worth around $1,000.

Due to the high costs of electricity to run computers on blockchain networks using this proof of work algorithm, there is an advantage for countries where electricity is cheap or for organizations that have special deals with energy companies.

As the difficulty of the puzzles on the Bitcoin blockchain increases so will the electricity consumption, making it even more costly and resource intensive to run a blockchain with proof-of-work algorithm on a large scale.

Lack of scalability

At the current rate of energy consumption, the electricity costs of running a blockchain using the proof-of-work algorithm make it unfeasible to handle the number of transactions by credit card companies like Visa and MasterCard. This is one of the factors that is currently affecting the scalability of blockchain networks.

A block is added to the Bitcoin blockchain every 10 minutes, each block currently contains around 2,000 transactions, meaning the Bitcoin network is processing around 3 transactions a second.

Due to block size limits, the Bitcoin network is only capable of handling around 7 transactions a second. Visa has conducted tests with IBM concluding the Visa network is capable of handling over 20,000 transactions a second.

If you go into a store and use your credit card but don't have enough money on the card to make the purchase, the credit card system will reject the transaction. The Bitcoin Blockchain has no mechanism in place like this.

A transaction on the Bitcoin blockchain will take a minimum of 10 minutes to be added the blockchain and companies may wait for several more blocks to be added before accepting the transaction, to ensure the transaction won't be reversed.

Comparing the difference between those two methods, if you were to go into a store to pay with Bitcoin, the store owner might have to wait an hour to ensure the transaction is confirmed with several blocks added to the blockchain on top of the block containing the transaction.

There are blockchain networks that are much faster than the Bitcoin network. However, none have the same level of popularity or acceptance as a form of payment as Bitcoin. Even the blockchains and cryptocurrencies that have faster transaction confirmation times still don't have the capacity to scale to the level of existing financial payment networks like Visa or MasterCard.

Due to these scalability issues, many people see the implementation of blockchain on a massive scale as nothing more than an official ledger of time-stamped information.

Trust, Reputation, and Understanding of Blockchains

There is still a lack of understanding about how the blockchain works along with a tarnished reputation from the connection with Bitcoin.

Bitcoin is the most commonly known use of the blockchain; many people have a strong association with Bitcoin and crime. While it is getting more mainstream acceptance as a legitimate payment method, terrorists, and computer crime bring Bitcoin back into the news reiterating that link.

A recent example is the computer networks at the National Health Service in the United Kingdom. A computer virus locked the computers of the NHS, preventing them from being accessed unless a ransom amount was paid in Bitcoin. This brought Bitcoin into the headlines in the UK, with newspapers linking Bitcoin to anonymous computer crime, hackers, and terrorists. Hospitals were unable to access patient records, potentially threatening the lives of people in need of medical care during this time.

The blockchain claims to create trust between people without the need to trust a third-party intermediary for transactions. However, people still need to trust in the blockchain network and the anonymous computers running it. It is hard to get people to trust a system that is used openly by criminals especially as many of the computers running the network are in foreign countries that are not regulated or controlled by their government.

Incidents of crime linked to Bitcoin are a reason that companies developing blockchain-based systems are trying to distance the connection between Bitcoin and the blockchain. The term "distributed ledgers" has become even more popular recently, to further create a gap between Bitcoin and new blockchain-based technologies.

The benefits of blockchain-based systems are difficult for many people to understand. As mentioned previously, many people already choose third-party intermediaries to access the blockchain, and they use standard passwords to log in on a website removing main benefits of blockchain technology. Many people don't like other people being able to see their balances or transactions or other aspects of the blockchain and prefer existing systems.

The public understanding, trust, and perception of blockchain networks will be important to mainstream acceptance of the technology. It may take a long time for the general public to trust blockchain networks and comfortably transact on them.

Regulation and Integration

"The world's biggest financial players and analysts are buzzing about an invention that became famous partly by promising to destroy them." - Mike Gault

Blockchain-based assets face a long process of regulation and integration issues with existing systems. Governments and banks are resistant to change due to the scale and cost of replacing existing systems.

Unless blockchain-based systems can prove they will provide significant cost savings or benefits to justify replacing existing systems, it's unlikely large institutions like governments or banks will use them anytime soon.

The government of Estonia is testing blockchain based systems, but Estonia has a population of less than 1.5 million. There are cities in the USA, China, and other countries with 10 times this population. While blockchain-based systems may work on a small scale, it's not as easy to integrate them on the scale needed for governments like the USA or large banks.

The R3 consortium and ripple are examples of blockchain-based or distributed ledgers that being integrated with many financial firms from different countries. There are financial companies that are withholding their transition over to using a blockchain-based ledger because of the "small" scale in which a blockchain has been tested.

If a large number of financial institutions move to a new, untested technology and are using it when issues are discovered, it could pose a very significant risk to financial markets and customer data.

There have also been concerns by the Financial Stability Oversight Counsel (FSOC) that some blockchain-based systems could be more vulnerable to fraud than is currently understood with small-scale testing.

Another issue with multiple financial institutions adopting a shared blockchain-based system or distributed ledger is the area in which regulators work. A blockchain-based system can theoretically span over many different regulatory jurisdictions and national boundaries, further darkening the waters between regulators and which jurisdiction a transaction should be handled by.

Large financial institutions will be wary about moving to any system where government regulation is unclear. The financial and business risks are too high if governments do not have clear regulations about how blockchain-based assets are treated. Regulation concerns, the cost of integration along with the lack of large-scale applications of blockchain-based systems will lead to a slow uptake in the technology from large financial institutions and governments.

Hype
A lot of writing about blockchain technology could be called evangelical or over-hyped, with claims that blockchain-based technology will change the world, disrupt governments, eliminate banks, solve world poverty, and perhaps give you rock hard ab-muscles without working out.

That last claim about the ab-muscles isn't true, but given the hype around blockchains, it wouldn't be surprising if there was a start-up in Silicon Valley pitching that idea to venture capital firms now.

It's easy to get caught in the hype of a new technology; the internet was no different. It was a revolutionary technology that has changed the world, but many of the predictions in the early days of the internet were "irrational exuberance."

The estimated timeframes about the impact of new technology vary dramatically and are often greatly underestimated. As mentioned in the history of blockchain chapter, DigiCash and other digital cash and cryptography-based technologies were around decades before Bitcoin but were too early in their predictions of market adoption of the technologies.

Even if many of the predictions about the impact of blockchain technology are accurate, they will not have any mainstream impact on society for years to come. The start-ups pioneering the technology now, may not be able to survive long enough to see their technology reach a mass market.

As mentioned earlier in this chapter, even when people want to use Bitcoin and blockchain-based systems, many still prefer the methods that the blockchain claims to replace instead. This eliminates the need for the blockchain-based systems in the first place if people prefer the existing systems over the supposed benefits of the blockchain.

Blockchain technology is just a new way of storing and managing data. It isn't the answer to all the world's problems, so don't believe all the hype.

Key Points:

Lack of Privacy – Many decentralized blockchains are not private. Account balances and transactions are accessible for anyone on the network to view.

Security Concerns – Blockchain-based assets are like cash—if you lose the cash in your wallet or it's stolen then it's gone. Many of the security methods in the blockchain will make mainstream adoption more difficult and perhaps less secure than existing methods as people write down private keys so they don't forget them.

No Centralized Control – With a decentralized blockchain network like Bitcoin, changes must be agreed to by a certain majority of the network, this may be over 50% but could be as high as 70% to 80% of the network. No single organization has control over the changes or direction of decentralized blockchains making them risky for businesses to use as they can't control any changes to the system.

Risk of 51% attack – Many computers that would run a worldwide blockchain would be in countries people are uncomfortable with historically due to crime, lax legal systems or lack of regulation. Low electricity and computer costs in these countries have led to large centers mining blocks on blockchains. If these data centers collaborated, they could potentially control over 50% of a network and take over control of it.

Unproven new technology – Blockchain technology is an unproven new technology that has mainly been applied to cryptocurrencies. There is still limited real-world software or companies using blockchain technology to prove it is beneficial to the existing systems.

Cost – It takes a substantial amount of energy to power. It is estimated that every half an hour the Bitcoin network uses the same amount of electricity as the average US household does in an entire year.

Note: Calculations about electricity consumption are based on the USA average home consumption of 10,000 to 12,000 kWh of electricity. This is the equivalent to the amount of electricity to generate 4 blocks on the Bitcoin blockchain.

Scalability issues – Blockchain networks have not yet been proven to scale effectively to the same level of existing systems. The Bitcoin network is only capable of handling around 7 transactions a second. However, the Visa network is capable of handling over 20,000 transactions a second.

Reputation and trust – Bitcoin is the most commonly known use of the blockchain, which has a strong connection with terrorism, drug dealing, and crime. People need to trust in the blockchain network they are using, especially if it replaces a trustworthy intermediary. Many people will be hesitant trusting blockchain networks that are also associated with criminal activities.

Lack of understanding about blockchain technology – How the blockchain works and the benefits of it are difficult for many people to understand. People also have concerns about aspects of blockchain networks such as their balances and transactions being public. Even if the benefits are understood, many people still prefer existing systems.

Regulation and integration – Blockchain-based systems will face regulation issues along with costly and time-consuming integration issues with existing systems. Governments and banks are resistant to change due to the scale and cost of replacing existing systems.

Hype – There is a lot of hype surrounding what blockchain-based systems are capable of. The blockchain is just a new type of database; it is not the magical solution is it often hyped up to be. It is also still unproven on a large scale or with many practical applications outside of cryptocurrencies.

Chapter Six: Blockchain and the Finance Industry

"Blockchain technology continues to redefine not only how the exchange sector operates, but the global financial economy as a whole."

– Bob Greifeld, Chief Executive of NASDAQ

Bitcoin was the first stable, worldwide use of blockchain technology and it quickly caught the attention of the finance industry. Many financial services companies didn't see much potential in Bitcoin until they examined it further and understood the blockchain technology behind it. Once they realized what blockchain-technology was capable of they poured millions of dollars into research, development, and acquisitions to develop their own blockchains.

Utilizing a blockchain-based technology in the world of finance has many upsides. Blockchain's ability to process information faster by eliminating intermediaries has the potential to drive down costs while increasing speed. This can be applied to currency transfers, stock trading, payments, settlements, and many activities that are at the core operations of financial institutions.

Transferring value is a slow process compared to the average length of financial transactions. It can sometimes take weeks to transfer money to certain countries with the exchange rate often uncertain at the time of transfer. A blockchain-based ledger can not only cut down the charge cost on the transfer of value, but it can also speed up the process significantly due to the removal of intermediary channels that information needs to pass through to validate transactions.

For banks, blockchain technology offers enhanced speed of transactions while replacing layers of authentication with transparency on transactions.

Banks settle transfers on internal ledgers; this may be done at different processing times for each bank. This often results in a transfer of funds removed from the ledger of one bank but not appearing on the ledger of another bank for days later.

In developing countries where settlements may be more manual, this could take much longer and is prone to error. Replacing this process with a blockchain would allow banks to almost instantly settle a transfer on a distributed ledger with everyone on the network able to see the transaction.

Share trading operates in much the same way. Blockchains can be utilized to cut down the time taken in the settlement process as well as heighten the accuracy of trades. In fact, the NASDAQ has already created a blockchain for share trading.

Currently, the blockchain that the NASDAQ is running is being used for pre-IPO share trades, transferring share ownership of private companies between investors before they are listed on the stock exchange. The NASDAQ blockchain is operational now, demonstrating how close the world is to having blockchain systems in many industries.

After the first transaction that transferred ownership of shares between investors, Bob Greifeld declared it a seminal moment in the application of blockchain technology and a major advance in the global financial sector.

No matter how great the potential benefits of blockchain technology, are financial institutions ready to implement this technology?

Are they willing to trust millions and potentially billions of dollars of transactions to be processed using blockchain technology?

The short answer is, yes.

The financial services industry is one of the first industries to accept the benefits that come with utilizing blockchain technology.

Many companies are already using blockchain technology, such as the NASDAQ example mentioned earlier. Almost every major financial institution in the world is currently involved in developing blockchain technology through internal development or joint ventures with other companies.

Nasdaq, Visa, Citibank, Capital One have invested over $30 million in chain.com to build distributed ledgers for transactions between financial institutions.

Ripple is a payment network that can be used to transfer different currencies, commodities or anything of value using distributed ledgers.

The Ripple payment network is being used by major banks and financial institutions around the world as a settlement network, allowing banks to send real-time international payments at a much lower cost than existing methods.

Currently, 15 of the world's top 50 banks are working with Ripple in developing the blockchain platform.

Paolo Cederle, CEO of UniCredit, is quoted as saying: "Blockchain and related technologies are a paradigm shift from the status quo and increasingly a major focus of innovation for us.

"Through our partnership with Ripple, we are optimizing our global payments as one of the first major banks to implement distributed financial technology in a commercial setting."

The tech firm R3 has been working with 25 major banks including Wells Fargo, JP Morgan, and Citibank. The companies involved in this project are known as the R3 consortium. R3 is a distributed database technology that has several high-profile developers from bitcoin core, cryptography and the tech industry working on it. The distributed ledger they created is different from a blockchain but does share many similarities. Eleven of the banks in the R3 consortium have already connected to the R3 distributed ledger.

Another prominent name that is developing blockchain technologies is The Bank of England. They said they would commit themselves to overhauling the foundations of their databases and implementing a blockchain. The Bank of England has a team dedicated to the blockchain, declaring it a key technological innovation.

The Bank of England hopes to utilize the technology to aid in its defense against a growing amount of cyberattacks, aiding their systems in allowing non-bank payments to settle transactions faster, and to make them more compatible with ever-changing technology

The Bank of England initially plans to use it internally, but they have promised to open the technology up to more businesses by 2020. If they stay true to their word, then blockchain-based technology will be tested on real-time gross settlement systems, handling hundreds of billions of banking transactions each day.

Estonia is another country that is implementing blockchain technology. The Estonian government is pioneering digital technology for government by developing blockchains for identification and health records with other areas such as tax collection with voting planned to potentially be built on the top of these foundations.

Blockchain technology is rapidly being adopted by the finance industry and central banks, but it is also becoming more popular with institutions outside of finance. The next chapter examines companies outside of finance that are utilizing this new technology to transform their industries.

Key Points:

- Transferring value between companies and countries is currently a slow process. Blockchain technology offers enhanced speed of transactions with the potential for real-time instant transfers.

- Blockchain technology can replace layers of authentication with the transparency of transactions.

- Many banks, central banks, governments, and financial companies are already utilizing blockchain technology or are currently researching and developing them.

- Share trading involves a transfer of ownership between people. Blockchains can be utilized to replace intermediaries and process trades with the Nasdaq already implementing a working blockchain.

- Many administrative and settlement functions performed by financial institutions are outdated and manual. These functions could potentially be replaced with blockchains and distributed ledgers.

Chapter Seven: Blockchain and Industries Other Than Finance

"Blockchain and related technologies are a paradigm shift from the status quo and increasingly a major focus of innovation for us."

Paolo Cederle, CEO of UniCredit Business Integrated Solutions

In the previous chapter, we looked at how the finance industry is rapidly adopting blockchain technology. While blockchain has a strong association with payments and transactions, due largely to its start with Bitcoin, the potential for blockchain technology is far greater than just payments and the finance sector.

Blockchain has the potential to change almost every industry in the world. The projects in development show the impact blockchain technology could have on everyday life.

In this chapter, we'll cover the potential uses of blockchain with examples of companies currently building blockchain-based systems.

Identity management and digital identities
Identity management utilizing blockchain technology is a key innovation that could pave the way for the security and foundation of other industries. If you can trust someone is who they claim to be, then you can connect that to a range of other applications.

Blockchain technology solves many existing issues with digital identities. Currently, it is relatively easy to set up fake identities or steal someone else's identity online. Passwords are not secure, and centralized databases are vulnerable to attack. Once a centralized database is attacked, it may provide access to all customer data stored on the system.

Blockchain-based identification systems provide digital signatures using cryptography. They are unique, irrefutable, secure, and almost impossible to duplicate or access without authorization.

Blockchain-based identification is a real possibility in the future with the Estonian government and companies such as ShoCard already building identity systems on the blockchain.

In the future, this could be used for digital Identities, passports, driver's licenses, residency permits, birth certifications, marriage certificates, and other forms of identification.

Digital Voting

After building the technology that allows digital identities and digital signatures, it is easy to authenticate someone's identity for a range of other transactions and actions online.

Digital voting is a technology that has failed to be implemented successfully across countries due to security risks and privacy concerns.

Estonia, Denmark, and Norway have experimented with digital voting; however, only Estonia has successfully run a large scale digital voting.

Denmark has used blockchain technology for small-scale voting with the Liberal Alliance, a political party in Denmark using a blockchain voting system in 2014.

By using a blockchain-based voting system, a voter could check that their vote was successfully sent, while still retaining their privacy and hiding their identity. It would also make voting more accessible to many people, potentially increasing voter participation in elections.

Healthcare and Medical Records

A blockchain provides a distributed ledger where when changes are made in one ledger all other copies are updated simultaneously. This ensures that everyone has the most recent valid data matching all copies on the network.

A lot of potential has been applied in the healthcare industry. If you've ever been to more than one doctor or hospital, you'll be aware that each time you visit a new doctor or hospital, it involves a lot of paperwork about your medical history, allergies, and other medical questions you may have completed several times before in other locations.

Storing this information on a shared database of health records would mean that doctors, hospitals, surgeons, nurses, and health professionals would have access to shared data about a patient. They would have the full details of medical records, saving time and assisting them to make more comprehensive decisions when treating a patient.

This could be potentially life-saving in the case of a patient being rushed into surgery. The records of any underlying health issues, blood type, allergies to certain medicines, emergency contacts, current medications they may be taking or other details would be instantly accessible when required.

The details of a patient's prior history of illness would also help complete the puzzle of what may be causing health issues in a patient. A visit to a doctor for one condition may not trigger a cause for alarm, but when combined with a visit to another doctor or health professional for a seemingly unrelated condition, these may signal the symptoms of a yet undiagnosed issue. Each health professional may have had only one of the symptoms providing them only part of the picture, but with the additional information, they can better diagnose the patient.

Health insurance companies could save significant amounts of money and time by having access to this database as well. If you are applying for health insurance, currently this requires a lot of questions and medical tests that can be quite invasive, time-consuming, and uncomfortable. By providing access to your health records to an insurer, they would have a complete picture of your health history and be able to make insurance decisions based on this information without the need for extensive tests and questions.

Companies such as Gem, Tieroim, and Philips Healthcare are currently working on blockchains for health records. Estonia is leading the way among countries in this area. The Estonian eHealth authority has been working with blockchain technology company Guardtime to put citizens' medical data into a secure blockchain database.

The Road Administration Authority of Estonia has been receiving digital medical certificates to ensure a person is fit to drive before renewing their license. This was previously a manual process for citizens but is becoming digitized and automated. In the future, the health records on the blockchain could be updated with information such as whether a person was fit to drive. Government departments would have access to this information and systems would automatically issue renewals based on the information in the blockchain health records.

A blockchain of health records offers benefits for the individual person as well as health professionals. Individuals will have a more transparent and accurate view of their medical records and health data. No government or company can change this information without the patient, along with everyone on the network, being aware of it.

Estonia has set up a patient portal, where citizens have full access to their medical history, prescriptions, referral details and insurance information. In the patient portal, they can also declare whether to be an organ donor and make decisions about their treatments during surgery.

In the future, this database of health records may all be on a blockchain. With Estonia rapidly leading the way, this may only be a few years away from being a reality.

Academic Certificates

The Holbertson School in California is planning to use blockchain technology to authenticate its academic certificates. Falsifying academic transcripts and certificates is a common practice with students claiming qualifications they didn't earn.

The blockchain would create transparency around students' academic records and qualifications. Allowing them to be easily verified, eliminating fraud while saving time and money to manually check or prove qualifications.

Music
The music industry is already developing blockchain based technology to use in a range of different ways. There are several companies that are developing blockchain based apps to change how music is distributed, shared, purchased and how royalties for sales will be paid to artists.

Peertracks, Uio Music, and Mycelia are just a few start-up companies that are working on blockchain-based platforms for artists to sell their music directly to their fans without the need for a record label or intermediary.

Spotify recently purchased Mediachain, which developed a blockchain-based system that allows artists to create digital records for songs on the Bitcoin blockchain and InterPlanetary File System. Spotify aims to utilize the blockchain platform from Mediachain to create fairer and more transparent payments to artists for their music.

Cloud Storage
Cloud storage companies like Google Drive, Dropbox, and Microsoft OneDrive have become the standard for storing data and files. Many people use cloud storage for storing all types of personal and business data.

Cloud storage currently requires a lot of trust in third-party companies. People often put all their data in one place, with one cloud storage company that only requires a low-security password to access. Centralized cloud storage systems are vulnerable to attack and passwords can easily be obtained through basic hacking or scamming methods.

There are several start-ups providing an alternative by combining cloud storage with blockchain technology.

Companies like Storj have created decentralized cloud storage that is less vulnerable to attacks and hacking. Cloud storage is distributed across unused storage space on computers connected to the network, it is encrypted and can only be accessed by the owner.

Siacoin and Filecoin are start-ups that are also working on combining cloud storage and blockchains like Storj.

Car Leasing and Rentals

The car industry is another industry that could be transformed by blockchain technology. Visa and DocuSign have already entered a partnership to develop a blockchain-based system for car leasing.

This would cut out a lot of the paperwork and intermediaries involved in car leasing. A customer selects the car they want to lease, their digital identity already contains finance and license information, they agree to an insurance policy for the lease and the blockchain is updated with the new lease agreement.

Short-term car rentals at airports are moving towards being more automated removing the need for lengthy paperwork and processes before renting a car. The technology being developed for car leasing and digital identities could also be applied to car rentals.

The medical records of many citizens in Estonia are already digitized and passed to the Road Authority to automatically renew licenses. This linking of blockchain information and digital identities could also be used to automatically approve car rentals in the future.

Ride-Sharing

Ride-sharing apps like Uber have disrupted the taxi industry and changed transport for millions of people around the world. Taxi companies had a monopoly over car transport in many cities around the world with one organization controlling all the taxi licenses for a city.

While Uber and other ride-sharing apps provided an alternative to Taxis, they are still centralized databases with systems all controlled by one company.

Ride-sharing is between the driver and passengers; however, with current ride-sharing platforms, there is still an intermediary between all interactions and ride transactions.

Blockchain technology would make it possible to remove any intermediary and create decentralized ride-sharing apps.

Start-up company La'zooz is currently working on a blockchain-based decentralized ride-sharing platform.

Ride-sharing is an industry that would be an easy adjustment to replace existing platforms with a blockchain.

Security of drivers would be a concern; however, once digital identities linked to road authority blockchains or car leasing and rental blockchains are common practice, ride sharing could integrate well with those blockchains.

Property

Property, real estate, and land sales are areas that currently involve a lot of manual paperwork and intermediaries to facilitate transactions. Property transactions involve records that are often difficult to obtain, prone to error, misplaced or a slow process.

Blockchain-based property records and transactions could dramatically increase the speed and transparency of property transactions while reducing the cost of transactions.

Real estate blockchain-based platforms could record land titles, transfer property deeds, track zoning changes or building plans and almost any property currently recorded by companies or local governments.

Ubiquity is a start-up currently building a blockchain-based property platform for banks, financial institutions, mortgage brokers, and regular people to track documents related to property transactions.

Apartment Rentals

Airbnb is another example of a platform like Uber that disrupted an industry by providing a platform that allowed people to rent their apartments to other people in cities around the world.

Airbnb removed intermediaries such as hotels and travel agents, bringing people together to transact with each other. While it is a step in the direction of removing intermediaries, it still just replaces intermediaries with another platform to facilitate transactions between people.

Blockchain-based hotel and apartment rental platforms may operate like Airbnb but without the intermediary facilitating all the transactions and bookings. These would be done directly between people on the blockchain.

Travel industry

Even more traditional hotel booking platforms could be replaced by blockchain-based booking systems.

John Guscic, the managing director of Webjet, states that "Around 1 in 25 hotel booking transactions around the world end where someone provides a service but doesn't get paid."

This is caused by the number of intermediaries involved in hotel and travel booking industry where bookings get lost or paid incorrectly. A blockchain-based booking system would create a more transparent booking system less prone to errors.

Webjet is currently working with Microsoft to develop a blockchain-based system for the travel industry; however, there is currently no timeframe on the release.

Loyalty / Rewards programs

Loyalty / Rewards programs are common with most industries, from the local coffee shop to major airlines. However, rewards programs are often expensive to run, prone to fraud, and customers often feel dissatisfied with the rewards received or process for checking balances and redeeming rewards.

Blockchain technology offers a solution to many issues facing existing loyalty / rewards programs. The financial services firm Deloitte published a paper titled "Making Blockchain Real For Customer Loyalty Rewards Programs" that examined how blockchain-based loyalty programs could benefit companies and customers.

The paper states that existing customer loyalty programs suffer from low client participation, slow processing times, fraud, and high costs to run. A blockchain-based loyalty program would be more transparent while significantly reducing processing times, costs, and increasing security.

When a transaction occurs that a customer would earn loyalty points for, it would be in real time as opposed to the slow processing time to credit balances to customers now. Companies could more seamlessly integrate loyalty programs allowing value-add opportunities to customers and potential business opportunities by sharing programs with complementary companies.

A start-up company called Loyyal has been working with major technology, accounting, and other companies on building a blockchain-based loyalty program. With the transparency, reduced costs, and improved speed comes better loyalty and rewards programs for companies and their customers.

Predictions and gambling

The gambling industry is set to be changed by emerging blockchain start-ups. It's not just gambling on sporting events that is set to change but the entire predictions industry, including predictions on financial markets and forecasting.

One of the fastest growing cryptocurrencies is Augur, which is developing a prediction market where people can predict and profit from the outcome of events.

Augur will be a decentralized platform for forecasting the probability of any event occurring. The system is based on research that shows that prediction markets have been proven to be more accurate over time than individual analysts, experts, surveys or opinion polls. In opinion polls, many people respond with what they want to happen in the outcome of an event, not what they think will happen. This is often why election results and polls can be completely inaccurate with the results being wildly different from opinion poll predictions. Prediction markets ask people to "put their money where their mouth is," as the saying goes, and risk money on the outcome of the event occurring which leads to more accurate results over time.

Smart Contracts

The examples in this chapter show that blockchain technology might be the next big innovation across a range of industries. These examples are just the tip of the iceberg in terms of what blockchain technology is capable of. Many of the applications of blockchain technology will be managing using smart contracts.

In the next chapters, we'll look at smart contracts, decentralized apps, the Ethereum platform, and other examples of what blockchain technology is capable of.

Key Points:

It is not just financial services companies implementing blockchain-based systems. Blockchain technology has a wide range of uses across different industries.

Blockchain-based technology can be used to transfer and record almost anything of value.

Many companies are already developing their own blockchain systems, with some blockchain-based systems already working and available now.

In the future, intermediaries and platforms may be replaced by blockchain platforms.

Blockchain technology is a much closer reality than many people may be aware of. In the next few years, there is likely to be a range of industries implementing blockchain technology.

Chapter Eight: Ethereum, Smart Contracts, and Decentralized Applications

"Giving users easy access to many different kinds of digital assets on the blockchain, particularly tokens that are linked to assets in the real world, is crucial to seeing blockchain adoption reach the next level...."

Vitalik Buterin Chief Scientist, Ethereum

Introduction to Ethereum

Ethereum is the next step in the future of blockchain technology. It is built from the same foundation technologies as the Bitcoin blockchain; however, it takes the possibilities of blockchain technology to another level.

Ethereum is a blockchain with a programming language that allows applications and smart contracts to run on top of the underlying blockchain.

This allows developers to create programs that run on a blockchain and use the computing power of thousands of computers connected to the blockchain network.

Almost any application that is running on a computer today could potentially run on a blockchain. By utilizing the Ethereum network, developers can quickly create applications with ease without the need to create their own blockchain and cryptocurrency.

The Ethereum network uses the cryptocurrency "Ether," which acts as currency on the network. Ether is exchanged as payment for running decentralized apps on the network.

The cryptocurrency Ether is the second largest cryptocurrency by market cap after bitcoin with a market cap over $10 billion dollars.

Difference between Ethereum and Bitcoin

The primary difference between Bitcoin and Ethereum is that Bitcoin is mainly used as a distributed ledger for financial transactions, but Ethereum is designed to be used as a distributed computing platform for running applications.

Bitcoin can be used to pay for goods and services anywhere they are accepted, the currency of the Ethereum network "Ether" is designed to be used by developers to pay for computing power on the network when running decentralized applications.

Bitcoin and Ethereum both have digital currencies but from an overall point of view, they differ in purpose. The point of Ether was not to establish itself as a payment alternative but to encourage developers to create and run applications within Ethereum.

To put it simply: Bitcoin is mainly a currency for financial transactions. Ethereum has multiple facets. While it does have its own cryptocurrency ("ether"), that is not all it has. The currency is one small part of the network as Ethereum also has an entire computing platform on top of the blockchain.

Benefits of Ethereum

As the Ethereum blockchain network is run by thousands of computers around the world, applications can be run using the computing power of a massive global network of computers.

One of the problems with the Bitcoin network is that it is more powerful than the top supercomputers in the world combined and yet that processing power is wasted generating random numbers to add blocks to the blockchain.

Ethereum puts all the computers connected to the network and their processing power to better use allowing developers to create applications that run using the combined processing power of the network along with blockchain technology.

Developers do not need to create their own blockchain and get computers to connect to it. Ethereum has an already established network of computers on the Ethereum blockchain.

The Ethereum platform also has the Ethereum Virtual Machine and Solidity programming language. Solidity can be used to create decentralized applications or smart contracts that are then compiled by the Ethereum Virtual Machine and run on the blockchain.

Decentralized Applications (dApps)
Decentralized Applications are applications that are open source, not controlled by one person or entity and run across a distributed blockchain or network of computers.

dApps have no central server. Instead, the users connect to each other through peer to peer connections.

With standard applications, they are controlled by one entity, run on a centralized server that is prone to hacking or downtime due to the server going offline.

A decentralized app has no single server or entity controlling it. It runs across a network of computers and changes are decided by the users.

There is no central point that the server could crash or be hacked. If one computer on the network goes offline, the application is unaffected as there are thousands of other computers the application is running from at the same time.

Even if one computer on the network is hacked, it can't make unauthorized changes to the application as the majority of the network must agree to the changes.

Smart Contracts
Smart contracts are contracts that are written in computer code and operate on a blockchain or distributed ledger.

They automatically verify, execute, and enforce the contract based on the terms written in the code. Smart contracts can be partially or fully self-executing and self-enforcing.

Smart contracts can be used to exchange anything of value, as mentioned in the chapter about potential uses of the blockchain, many of the industries utilizing blockchain technology will be using smart contracts.

When a smart contract is run on the blockchain, it operates automatically. If the conditions of a contract are met, payments or value are exchanged based on the terms of the contract. Likewise, if conditions in the contract are not met, payments may be withheld if written into the smart contract.

Smart contracts run as they are programmed on a decentralized network of computers on the blockchain removing risks around unauthorized changes, fraud, server failure or non-compliance with the terms of the contract. The contracts execute automatically, exchanging value and payments between people without the need for lawyers or courts to enforce them.

Entries on the blockchain are timestamped and can't be altered. This creates an ideal platform for contracts as any changes to contracts are timestamped, while the previous versions are retained on the blockchain.

Contracts can be stored (and new versions created) all the while preserving former copies (as well as accurate timestamps on all edits and revisions). It not only gives a more accurate outline of the processes that took place but it also makes all parties involved more honest about the transactions taking place because the ledger can't be altered. The blockchain network removes the need for third-party intermediaries for managing the contracts.

Uses of smart contracts

A risk with the Bitcoin network is that if you purchase an item using Bitcoin, after making the payment there is no guarantee you will receive the goods purchased. The other person involved could decide not to deliver the goods or claim they didn't receive the payment.

As there is no third-party intermediary for transactions on the Bitcoin network, traditional courses of action such as disputing the transaction, requesting a refund or contacting the intermediary are not possible.

Bitcoin wallets are also anonymous, so you may have no information about where the transaction was sent to. If a transaction was sent to the wrong address, then it is gone and the money is lost.

Smart contracts solve a lot of the risks associated with transacting on the blockchain network. Smart contracts can be used for anything of value that can be exchanged, and there are a lot of companies developing blockchain-based decentralized applications that utilize smart contracts.

Ascribe is a start-up in the art industry that allows many different artists to claim ownership over their work and issue limited-edition prints. The platform issues numbered artwork in its digital form and uses a blockchain to trace back all original creations and transactions within those creations. It has a marketplace where artists can advertise, and people can buy and sell art through their website.

UProov is a legal and media company that provides verifiable, real-time stamps on any and every video and picture taken on any electronic device. Pictures and videos with timestamps that can't be altered could be relied upon more heavily as evidence in court cases.

BitProof, another company that uses a blockchain to create timestamps, has an app that is easily downloadable onto a phone. This enables verifiable timestamps onto every piece of documentation you run through it. It can be traced back to its creation on a blockchain that cannot be altered. This technology could potentially eliminate the need for notaries in the future.

Warranteer is another company that already has ties to GoPro and LG. They use smart contracts to move product warranties onto a blockchain where it is easily accessible, transferable, and preserved. All traces of edits, changes, updates, and shifts are recorded onto a blockchain that both the warrantor and the warrantee can access at any given moment.

Peertracks, Mycelia, and Ujo Music are separate companies all focusing on using blockchain technology within the music industry. All three companies are using smart contracts in different ways with the main goals of removing intermediaries such as record labels, making it easier for musicians to sell directly to fans and get paid for their music.

Microfinance involves the lending of small sums of money, primarily in poorer countries around the world. These amounts are small to the banks; however, they are significant to the borrower, as it allows them to start a business, earn an income, and support their families.

Microfinance has lifted millions of people around the world out of poverty, helped by Mohamed Yunus, who won a Nobel Prize for his work with microfinance. Before the modernization of microfinance by Mohamed Yunus, most banks would not finance small loans as the paperwork cost more than the profit from the loan.

Micro-Insurance is an area that has not seen as dramatic a change as micro-lending. Start-up company Stratumn aims to change micro-insurance by working with Lemonway on the creation of a micro-insurance blockchain-based system called "LenderBot." LenderBot will use smart contracts on top of a blockchain to create and manage micro-insurance contracts.

When discussing the future of the Blockchain, the term "Blockchain 2.0" is commonly used to describe the next step in the evolution of blockchain technology. Decentralized apps along with smart contracts take the capabilities of blockchain technology to exciting new levels. The future of the blockchain will revolve around smart contracts and dApps. Blockchain 2.0 could potentially have an impact on the world exponentially greater than the impact Bitcoin and the original blockchain technology have had.

Key Points:

- Ethereum is a platform on top of a blockchain with a programming language that allows developers to create and run decentralized applications and smart contracts on the powerful, distributed computing platform and blockchain underlying the Ethereum platform.

- The Bitcoin currency and network is primarily used for financial transactions. Ethereum has a currency "Ether," but it is designed to be exchanged for computing power, not for financial transactions outside of the Ethereum platform.

- Decentralized apps (dApps) have no single server or entity controlling them; dApps run across a network of computers.

- Smart contracts are contracts that are written into computer code and operate on a blockchain or distributed ledger.

- Smart contracts automatically verify, execute and enforce the contract based on the terms written in the code without the need for third-party intermediaries such as lawyers or courts to enforce the contracts.

- Anything of value can be exchanged using smart contracts; they do not only refer to legal contracts. Smart contracts reduce risks associated with transacting on the blockchain network, as transactions and payments are handled automatically by the network.

- There are many companies already developing blockchain-based decentralized applications and smart contracts on the Ethereum platform.

- The Ethereum platform is the next step in the future of blockchain technology that includes smart contracts and decentralized apps—this technology is often referred to as "Blockchain 2.0."

Chapter Nine: The Future of Blockchain

"In the future, I see a public blockchain - whether that's Bitcoin or some other open one in the future, which is a way of registering ownership of all sorts of assets and it's a way of transferring ownership of those assets in a single system that can be read by all of the right people and none of the wrong people.

It becomes very simple for me to swap my dollars for your IBM shares, or your pounds for my house. Any asset that we assign a value to and want to be sure about who owns it can be registered using this technology."

- James Smith, CEO of Elliptic

As discussed in this book, blockchain technology has the potential to reach every country, industry, and person on the planet within the next few decades. Many of the predictions about the future of blockchain technology are assumptions; however, these are not predictions like "in the future, there will be flying cars." There are many blockchain-based systems are already in development in many industries.

The momentum that blockchain technology has gained over the last few years in terms of investment in corporate and government projects makes the prediction of a future with blockchain technology incorporated into our daily lives very realistic.

If we look at the current blockchain-based systems being created, the industries they are being used for and the trends that are appearing, we can expand those trends into the future to get an idea of the future direction of blockchain-based systems.

Open source decentralized vs closed source centralized

A current divide in blockchain development is whether blockchains should be decentralized with the source code publicly available (open source) or centralized with the source code privately held by an organization or group of collaborators (closed source).

The original components of blockchain technology believe blockchains should be open source and decentralized. Companies and governments see the decentralized, open source blockchain technologies and think it is brilliant however they just want it without the decentralized and open source aspects.

This is like the early days of personal computing where most programmers believed that software should be open source and free to everyone. Bill Gates received a lot of criticism for going against this mindset by turning software into a business where it was licensed and sold. While open source software is still popular, most software companies these days do not share their code openly.

Ripple is one of the most well-known blockchain projects and currently the third largest cryptocurrency by market capitalization. Ripple is closed source and centralized; it is distributed among a select group of financial institutions as a distributed ledger for settling transactions between them.

Ripple receives a lot of criticism from the open source community that does not want the future of blockchain technology to consist of closed, centralized blockchains owned by large financial institutions.

Ethereum is the second largest cryptocurrency by market capitalization and one of the largest blockchain network. Ethereum is open source and decentralized; it provides a platform for developers to build decentralized applications with tokens on the blockchain using the Ethereum platform.

There does not appear to be a clear winner that blockchain-based systems will take between open sourced decentralized and closed source distributed/centralized blockchains. There is significant development work and funding for both methods as each has benefits that suit different requirements, organizations, and communities.

Blockchain technology will likely continue to move in both directions of open source decentralized networks along with closed source centralized networks simultaneously. Governments and large corporations will choose one method while individual programmers, small-scale projects, and start-ups will choose another.

Distributed ledgers

The R3 consortium of major financial institutions is another direction that companies are taking. This consortium was originally developing a blockchain; however, it has moved to a distributed ledger. While the R3 consortium distributed ledger has many of the benefits of the blockchain, it is not a blockchain.

Distributed ledgers are currently heavily associated with blockchain, and it is assumed that a distributed ledger is blockchain-based. However, distributed ledgers can operate without using the blockchain.

Most development work and start-ups are blockchain-based however distributed ledgers not based on the blockchain could be a trend that emerges in the future.

Fewer cryptocurrencies

At the start of any developing industry, there are many companies. However, as the industry and market develop, this number reduces until there are only a few major corporations or brands left.

At the start of the 1900s when cars were a new technology, there were thousands of car manufacturers in the USA, now there are only a few major companies manufacturing cars.

This rate of reduction in car manufacturers is common among most industries and will likely prove to be the trend among cryptocurrencies in the future. Currently, there are thousands of cryptocurrencies with more being created each day. In the future, it's likely that only a few major cryptocurrencies will remain and receive mainstream acceptance as a form of payment.

This trend is already occurring as new blockchain projects are launching using tokens on existing blockchains such as Ethereum instead of creating their own cryptocurrencies.

More blockchain tokens

While there will likely be a reduction in the number of cryptocurrencies, the number of tokens on blockchain platforms will increase.

Tokens are like cryptocurrencies as they are exchanged on the blockchain for purchases. However, they run on top of an existing blockchain, with the token representing value issued on top the currency of another blockchain.

Ethereum is the most popular blockchain for this concept. The Ethereum blockchain uses a native currency called "Ethers." Anyone can issue tokens on top of the Ethereum blockchain, the tokens represent value and are used as a means for exchange but utilize the existing Ethereum blockchain and Ethers currency.

Tokens allow developers and organizations to create applications that run on a blockchain without having to create and maintain their own blockchain or cryptocurrency.

Blockchain 2.0 - Decentralized apps (dApps) and Smart Contracts

Blockchain 2.0 is the term to describe the new functionality of the blockchain that exists now compared to the original source code.

The Ethereum platform made it possible to create and run decentralized apps and smart contracts on a blockchain. dApps, Smart Contracts and the Ethereum platform were covered in detail earlier in the book.

dApps and smart contracts built on the Ethereum network or other existing blockchains that use tokens instead of cryptocurrencies is a rapidly growing new trend that shows no signs of slowing down.

More regulation and acceptance

There is still significant criticism and concerns about blockchain technology. Bitcoin is an example of this; governments claim transactions are too private, making it easy to use for criminal activities, money laundering, and tax evasion. On the other side of that argument, people claim that the decentralized database like Bitcoin, the openness of being able to see anybody's wallet, current balance and transactions make it too transparent and not private enough.

Many of the criticisms are due to Bitcoin being the most well-known, worldwide, mainstream and viable application of blockchain technology. Blockchain is still in its early days. It is very heavily associated with Bitcoin and cryptocurrencies, and there are hundreds of open source cryptocurrencies being created each month.

Governments previously dismissed Bitcoin viewing it as only used by criminals and money laundering. That view has started to change as blockchain technology is better understood and the financial institutions are integrating the technology into financial markets. Governments are now encouraging Financial Technology (FinTech) companies to do business in their country, accepting cryptocurrencies as a new form of payment and ensuring it is regulated correctly within the country.

Japan recently legalized Bitcoin as a legal form of payment, Australia recently removed taxes on cryptocurrencies along with encouraging companies involved with blockchain-based technologies to do business in Australia.

Governments will continue to try to attract start-ups in the FinTech space working with banks, companies, and financial institutions to create jobs, promote commerce, and grow the economy through new blockchain-based technologies.

Blockchains in everyday life

Whether open source decentralized applications are built on existing blockchains or new private consortium blockchains are created, there will be an increase in the number of blockchains used in every area of our lives.

Many company and government databases using outdated spreadsheets or manual ledgers will be replaced by blockchains. Major banks around the globe are already developing their own blockchains to handle transactions, ledger entries, exchanges between currencies and more.

The utilization of blockchain technology may continue to grow until it is as common as today's database technology used by companies and governments. There will also be a trend of blockchain alternatives to existing industry options in everyday life.

An example showing the trend of blockchain alternatives existing alongside existing options is cloud storage. Storj and Siacoin are companies that are creating decentralized cloud-based storage on the blockchain. While they are unlikely to replace Google Drive or Dropbox anytime soon, they have provided an alternative option when deciding where to store files in the cloud.

The hype about blockchain-based systems disrupting existing industries and replacing companies may not come true in the short term, but there is a clear trend that in many industries blockchain-based alternatives will exist alongside existing options.

Blockchain technology may not replace existing intermediaries like banks or companies like Google or Uber as some people have predicted, especially not in the short term. However, even if intermediaries aren't replaced, you will eventually encounter blockchain technologies through distributed blockchain ledgers at work, smart contracts, decentralized applications or being able to choose a blockchain-based alternative to current options in many areas of everyday life.

Key Points:

- **Open source decentralized vs. closed source centralized** – There is no clear winner for the future direction of development yet. Both open source decentralized blockchains will be developed alongside closed source centralized/consortium blockchains to suit different requirements.

- **Distributed ledgers:** Distributed ledgers that do not use a blockchain but have many of the benefits of a blockchain is a trend that may compete with blockchain based ledgers in the future.

- **Fewer cryptocurrencies and more blockchain tokens:** A trend that is currently occurring is companies using tokens on the Ethereum platform instead of their own blockchains and cryptocurrencies. This trend looks set to continue as the functionality of the Ethereum platform allows development of Decentralized Apps and Smart Contracts.

- **Blockchain 2.0:** Blockchain technology now has significantly increased functionality such as Decentralized apps (dApps) and Smart Contracts that were not part of the original blockchain code. Blockchain 2.0 is used to refer to the future of blockchain technology including these enhancements to separate it from the original blockchain capabilities.

- **More regulation and acceptance:** Governments and companies have moved towards accepting cryptocurrencies as legitimate forms of payment along with investing heavily in blockchain infrastructure and technology.

- **Blockchain in everyday life:** Even if the blockchain-based technology isn't as revolutionary as predicted, it still looks set to become a part of every life through distributed ledgers, payment options or software alternatives for existing options.

Chapter Ten: Technical Guide to the Blockchain

Introduction to the technical guide to the blockchain
This technical guide to how the blockchain works is at the end of the book as it may not interest many readers. This section will cover the more advanced aspects such as hashes and cryptography involved in the blockchain.

If you are not interested in the cryptography behind the blockchain then you can skip this section or come back to it later.

There are some resources and a glossary of terms after this chapter that provide further details about the blockchain, Bitcoin, Ethereum and smart contracts that may be also be of interest.

Technical guide to how the blockchain works
This guide will focus on how the Bitcoin blockchain works as this was the original blockchain and all other blockchains are based on this foundation so will work in a similar way.

The Bitcoin blockchain uses the SHA-256 algorithm. The SHA-256 algorithm generates unique, fixed-size 256-bit hash. A hash is like a secret code that uses an encryption method that hides data in a way that makes it almost impossible to decrypt without authorization.

The hash generated is always the same length. It doesn't matter whether you put one word or an entire book, you will still get a hash of the same length for any amount of data entered.

If you change one of the letters then the hash will completely change. The hash appears to be random with no connection to the data entered. It is almost impossible to figure out the original message from the hash unless you know the original message or have a private key.

Some examples of hashes generated from different words and phrases are below:

The hash of the word "Blockchain" with upper case B:
b3f4e9b8455ea3ea20e60aae2cad91d8412a53bc4f3834e3152f776e
b4b44d4c

The hash of the word "blockchain" with lower case b:
154a5318f688615ba779541d8753e0b7047f5ba4b5cd7676d124008
201803e73

The hash of the word "block chain" with a space between the words "block" and "chain":
7ef554758e1810b1dec1f43ef6c2d0ff105b63987561fdb4f352d9433d
231457

This is the entire play of Shakespeare's "Romeo and Juliet" containing over 20,000 words:
e807d23c1ff8e4ba4aa4542d35082e28f9f580407ca6031a34bc1eff4
24fd37a

From the examples above, you can see that it is impossible to tell the input data from the hash generated. It's also clear that a small change, such as changing a letter from uppercase to lower case, or adding a space will significantly change the hash generated.

Hashing transactions into blocks

The previous examples were to show how the hash generated has no detectable pattern to the length of text or type of data entered. The examples above don't contain transactions, so for the next example we'll use transactions and convert them to hashes. After the hashes are generated we'll link them in a blockchain.

The first block in the blockchain is block 0, also known as the genesis block.

Block 0

The first block of transactions will contain the text:
"John receives 100 bitcoins

Sally receives 50 bitcoins
Sam receives 10 bitcoins"

Hash 0 =
0000641727781545e50c0235823c9ae0785d419499cc5a5dcdff233
2a53f0f7f

Block 1
The second block of transactions will contain the transactions
below:
John sends Sally 50 bitcoins
Sally sends Sam 10 bitcoins

Each transaction will be signed with a private key by the owner of
the sending Bitcoin address. The network won't be able to see the
private key but they can verify the correct private key authorized to
send the bitcoins was used.

The block will also contain the hash of the previous block:
0000641727781545e50c0235823c9ae0785d419499cc5a5dcdff233
2a53f0f7f

A number known as a "nonce" (Number used Once) will also be
included. The nonce is the answer to the puzzle that miners must
solve to add a valid block to the blockchain and earn rewards.

Hash 1 =
0000ed29ee4097b79e194adb355b18c500a900ffb3a1670dec4673e
ac2abdd07

Block 2
The third block of transactions will contain the signed transactions
below, along with the hash of the previous block and the nonce:
Sally sends Sam 20 bitcoins
John sends Sally 20 bitcoins

Hash 2 =
0000d5cada28a39cb0511cc871d550fe0c4ba704a93ad33db378936
c6ab40caf

Block 3:

The forth block of transactions will contain the signed transactions below, along with the hash of the previous block and the nonce:

Sam sends John 10 bitcoins
Sally sends John 20 bitcoins

Hash 3 =
00001bbd6491304360d142bd5f32610214937c263b0bc6c44b3ac04
574b62d4c

Creating a blockchain

Using those examples above, we have 4 pieces of data that have been converted to hashes. We can now add those hashes into blocks and create a blockchain that links them.

The first block on the blockchain will have the hash:
0000641727781545e50c0235823c9ae0785d419499cc5a5d
cdff2332a53f0f7f

This is "block 0" or the "genesis block", there is no previous block on the blockchain that this block needs to reference.

The second block on the blockchain will be "Block 1" and will reference the hash of the genesis block.

Each block added to the blockchain will reference the hash of the block before in the header, linking them together like a chain. Using the transaction examples above, we can create a blockchain that looks like the below:

Block 0 – Genesis block:

Hash of previous block: 0 – no previous block

Hash of block 0:
0000641727781545e50c0235823c9ae0785d419499cc5a5d
cdff2332a53f0f7f

Block 1:

Hash of previous block (Block 0):
0000641727781545e50c0235823c9ae0785d419499cc5a5d
cdff2332a53f0f7f

Hash of block 1:
0000ed29ee4097b79e194adb355b18c500a900ffb3a1670d
ec4673eac2abdd07

Block 2:
Hash of previous block (Block 1):
0000ed29ee4097b79e194adb355b18c500a900ffb3a1670d
ec4673eac2abdd07

Hash of block 2:
0000d5cada28a39cb0511cc871d550fe0c4ba704a93ad33d
b378936c6ab40caf

Block 3:
Hash of previous block (Block 2):
0000d5cada28a39cb0511cc871d550fe0c4ba704a93ad33d
b378936c6ab40caf

Hash of block 3:
00001bbd6491304360d142bd5f32610214937c263b0bc6c4
4b3ac04574b62d4c

That's a basic example of the creation of the blockchain. Each group of transactions is converted into a hash, combined with the hash of the previous block and a number that the miners solve. The hash is included in the header of the next block linking each new block to the block before it.

We can follow the transactions from the current block, all the way back to the very first block to understand what has occurred on the blockchain.

Altering the blockchain
As we saw in the first example of generating hashes, any minor change to the text will generate an entirely different hash.

This is how the blockchain makes it almost impossible to commit fraud by altering transactions in previous blocks.

In block 1, it contains the transactions below:
John sends Sally 50 bitcoins
Sally sends Sam 10 bitcoins

If Sam wanted to manipulate the blockchain and alter that transaction so Sally sends him 20 bitcoins instead of 10. It would only be a minor change of changing 1 number within that transaction.

This kind of alteration could easily occur in current financial databases, where one number is accidently or deliberately entered incorrectly and goes unnoticed.

With the blockchain, changing this one number creates an entirely new hash for that block of transactions.

The original hash of the block is:
0000ed29ee4097b79e194adb355b18c500a900ffb3a1670d ec4673eac2abdd07

The new hash of the block would be:
0000f3e9eda5e3f8782c5051068935abcd710ffd5fecb7fe7e aa6a57f8aa1208

As each block in the blockchain links to the previous block, the header hash in block 2 would need to be changed so it includes the new hash of block 1 with the altered transaction.

This would change the hash of block 2, which would mean header hash of block 3 would need to change to reference the new hash of block 2.

This would continue all the way to the most recent block on the blockchain until all the hashes of the blocks had been changed.

Confirmations on the blockchain
A new block is added every 10 minutes on the Bitcoin blockchain. Many other blockchains add a block faster than this. To change a transaction included in a block, each block would have to be re-mined with new hashes faster than the rest of the network is adding blocks.

This may be possible for a few of the most recent blocks, however it is generally accepted that once 6 blocks have been added on top of a block of transactions, it becomes computationally impossible to alter transactions in that block.

A new block added on top of a previous block, is considered a confirmation that the previous block of transactions is valid and won't change. 6 blocks on top would be 6 confirmations and enough confidence that the transactions before those 6 blocks won't be altered or reversed.

Blockchain network difficulty target
The hashes provided in the transaction example have several zeros in front of them. A block can only be added to the Bitcoin blockchain if the hash is lower than the target hash of the network.

The below examples might be a bit technical, but think of it like randomly rolling a dice. A dice has the numbers 1 to 6 on it, if you select the number 6 as the target, then if anyone rolls a dice and gets below the number 6 then they can add a block to the blockchain.

The lower the target number, the more difficult it becomes to randomly roll a lower number as there are less accepted options. If the target number is 2, then only someone that rolls the number 1 can add a block to the blockchain. This would take a lot longer to randomly roll this number, so as the number of people rolling dice increases, the number is reduced to keep the rate of adding blocks to the blockchain consistent.

In the example blockchain created earlier, the hash of block 3 has four zeros in front of it as shown below:
00001bbd6491304360d142bd5f32610214937c263b0bc6c4 4b3ac04574b62d4c

If the network target is five zeros and the number 5, e.g. 000005, then a hash is only valid if it is lower than 000005, otherwise it wouldn't be accepted as a valid block on the blockchain.

Example Target hash:
000005d6b56a86dd37a43d070fe7eb7e59cf6026f7f1f5f142 86f11a3ab151c9

Example acceptable hashes:

Five zeros and the number 4:
000004e13ccc4e31d500b52bc226dc4abb4627c383beaef6f 4da90a61b7994f0

Seven zeros and a number:
0000000022b64fdf30dd4f28a50b542345b9750ee24a346742 3acdb66dea27e4ff55

Eight zeros and a number:
000000004a4a2e623f745df50e97e62c9e854d07b0eef79a0 7ddad848c780133

Example rejected hashes:

Three zeros and a number:
0005f765f3c32e5e911ca18e136746daa0befff8a6d7aa48fa 487debd959a69d507f

Four zeros and a number:
00001c8d7349aea0dd4acf2d16cb5f575035a9ea80b080f75 1c832dfb97223043ab3f

Five zeros and the number 6:
000006a3842a3742929149840eb13f8343bb9c332a1c95e9 c20f9e20692fe45e24f

This is a more advanced version of the rolling the dice example, but the same logic applies with a much greater set of numbers.

Mining blocks

The nonce is the number that is included in the block that when it is hashed will generate a hash that is lower than the target making it acceptable to be included in the blockchain.

A number that creates a valid hash that is lower than the current network target is the puzzle that miners are trying to solve to add a block to blockchain and earn rewards.

The miners select the outstanding transactions to be included in the next block to be added to the blockchain along with matching transaction inputs and outputs. Also included is the hash of the previous block, current network difficulty target, merkle tree root, the blockchain address to pay the reward to and timestamp.

When adding transactions to a block, a miner can select any combination of outstanding transactions that are waiting to be added to the blockchain. Usually they will select the transactions with the highest fees attached to them as the miners receive the fees along with the block reward if they successfully add a block to the block chain.

As shown in the examples above, the hash generated seems random and appears to have no connection to the data entered. The miners don't know what the hash will be until they generate the hash.

They can only add a block to the blockchain if the hash they generate is lower than the network hash target. To achieve this, they add a number along with the transactions and hash of the previous block then generate a hash.

If the hash generated is lower than the network target, they can add it to the blockchain. If it is higher than the network target, they change the nonce (number) and try again. There is no way to determine what the hash will be, so the process of generating the number is just random guesses.

The miner that finds a number that when combined with outstanding transactions creates a hash lower than the network target can add a block to the blockchain.

The miner that adds a valid block to the blockchain, receives the transaction fees and block reward.

Once the number is found, all other computers on the network can add that number to the transaction data and confirm it is correct. This random number is difficult to find, but easy to verify it is correct once it is found.

The valid block is added to the blockchain and then all the computers on the network update their system with the latest version of the blockchain including the new block.

Miners then repeat this process to try and add the next block to the blockchain faster than the other miners on the network.

Increasing network difficulty

The process of finding the correct number that makes a valid hash is a random game of chance, like the example of rolling the dice. Processing speed plays a big factor as the faster a computer can guess the numbers the quicker it can find the correct answer.

The Bitcoin network is designed to add a block to the blockchain every 10 minutes. As more computers are added to the network, there is more processing power on the network making more guesses at the possible correct number for each block. To ensure the block time remains at approximately 10 minutes, the difficulty target is adjusted every 2,016 blocks adjusting the minimum and maximum numbers to add a valid block.

To go back to the dice example, a valid block may only be added if a person rolls a dice below the number 3. If one person is rolling a dice, they have a 2 in 6 chance of rolling a number below 3 which would below the network target of 3 and allow them to add a block to the blockchain.

For example, this may take them around 10 minutes to roll the number 1 or 2, so the network target of adding a block every 10 minutes is maintained. However, if another person is added to the network, also rolling a dice to get below the number 3, it may half the time taken to randomly roll the number 1 or 2, also halving the time taken to add a block to the blockchain.

To adjust for the increase in people on the network adding blocks faster than every 10 minutes, the network would adjust the target from 3 to 2, so a valid block is only accepted if it is below the number 2.

There was a 2 in 6 chance of getting a valid number, but the number of people doubled on the network, so the difficulty was lowered and is now 1 in 6 chance of getting a valid number. This would double the time it takes to get this target, which would adjust the block time added to the network back to 10 minutes.

The Bitcoin blockchain operates in a similar manner, as more computers are added to the network, the difficulty is adjusted by lowering the network target. Meaning there are less valid hashes that will be accepted and a wider range of numbers that need to be guessed to create a block with a valid hash.

Issues with proof-of-work

This method of calculating the correct number that makes a hash valid is known as "proof-of-work", as it demonstrates that computing power and resources were contributed to the network when adding a block.

Miners are rewarded for contributing computer power, electricity and resources to the network with payments for each block they successfully add to the network. This is known as the "block reward", the miners also receive the transactions fees for every block they add which is why they tend to select transactions with higher fees.

The proof-of-work method requires a large amount of computing power and electricity. The Bitcoin network is over 10,000 times more powerful than the world's top 500 supercomputers combined, yet most of that computing power is directed towards the purpose of generating random numbers.

The main issue with this method is that it is a massive waste of resources to perform a function that seems pointless and isn't required for a blockchain network to run.

Think about that for a second, there is a computer network that is more powerful than the world's most powerful supercomputers combined. Instead of working on potentially world changing problems, it is being utilized to randomly generate numbers. It seems a bit ridiculous which is why many people are critical of the wastefulness of the "proof-of-work" used by the Bitcoin blockchain.

There are other methods such as "proof-of-stake", "proof-of-capacity", "proof-of-activity" and "proof-of-burn" that can be used instead. These methods won't be covered in further detail, but it is important to be aware that there are alternatives to proof-of-work that are used by other blockchains.

The Ethereum platform utilizes the network to run decentralized apps, putting the computing power to better use. Ethereum is also moving away from proof-of-work and towards proof-of-stake on the Ethereum blockchain.

Security of the blockchain network

One of the significant security features of a decentralized blockchain is that everyone has access and all copies are updated across the network.

This plays a big part in ensuring that there is no central database where the blockchain can be manipulated by someone wanting to commit fraud.

Anyone can add a block to the blockchain but the majority of users on the network must accept it as valid.

Once a new block is accepted as valid, it is added to the blockchain, all the copies of the blockchain are updated across the network and the next block will be added on top of that.

If a person attempts to manipulate the transactions, it won't match the rest of the copies of the blockchain and so won't be accepted by the network.

51% attack and forks in the blockchain

A 51% attack was mentioned earlier in this book, it is a theoretical case where a user manages to control over 50% of the network. By controlling over 50%, they would then be able to decide which transactions and blocks were valid and the rest of the network would be updated with their version of the blockchain.

A fork is a situation where a large number of users on the network disagree with a change in the network, this could be the transactions and blocks added or the functionality of the network.

This disagreement creates a fork in the blockchain where some of the users split off and allocate their computing power to running a new blockchain that is separate from the original blockchain.

Major forks in blockchains have occurred with Ethereum and other cryptocurrencies. "Ether" and "Ether classic" are two separate blockchains there were created out of the original Ethereum blockchain, however due a disagreement, part of the Ethereum network split off and allocated resources towards a different version of the blockchain.

Summary

This chapter should have provided a more technical understanding on how a blockchain works.

There is some additional advanced information about blockchain networks available in the resources section of the next chapter.

If you enjoyed this book, found issues or wanted to get in contact:

If you enjoyed reading this book, it would be greatly appreciated if you were able to take a few moments to share your opinion and post a review on Amazon.

www.wisefoxpub.com/blockchain

I would be very grateful for you in your support if you found this book useful.

If you have any feedback, found any errors in the book or just wanted to get in contact to say hi, please feel free to email me at: mark@wisefoxpub.com

Thank you for reading this book, I hope you have found the information useful and it helps introduce you to blockchain technology.

See you on the blockchain!

Bonus Blockchain Resource Guide

Get the free Blockchain resource guide in digital format.

The guide includes the glossary of terms from this book in digital format.

It also includes continuously updated resources to learn more about Blockchain, Bitcoin, Ethereum and ICOs.

You can get the guide from the link below:
www.wisefoxbooks.com/resources

Resources and references

This section contains some resources and references relating to blockchain and Bitcoin. These were either referenced in the book or provide more detailed information about the history or technical details of blockchain technology.

A continuously updated PDF version of blockchain resources can be obtained for free at: **www.wisefoxbooks.com/resources**

History of blockchain and Bitcoin

Satoshi Nakamoto's original paper about Bitcoin, titled "Bitcoin: A Peer-to-Peer Electronic Cash System": *https://bitcoin.org/bitcoin.pdf*

Original Source Code for Bitcoin on GitHub: https://github.com/trottier/original-bitcoin/

Some of the first references to the "block chain" from the comments of the original Bitcoin source code:

// The basic transaction that is broadcasted on the network and contained in

// blocks. A transaction can contain multiple inputs and outputs.

// A transaction with a bunch of additional info that only the owner cares

// about. It includes any unrecorded transactions needed to link it back

// to the block chain.

// Nodes collect new transactions into a block, hash them into a hash tree,

// and scan through nonce values to make the block's hash satisfy proof-of-work

// requirements. When they solve the proof-of-work, they broadcast the block

// to everyone and the block is added to the block chain. The first transaction

// in the block is a special one that creates a new coin owned by the creator

// of the block.

// The block chain is a tree shaped structure starting with the

// genesis block at the root, with each block potentially having multiple

// candidates to be the next block.

Documents on work before Bitcoin that contributed to the creation of Bitcoin and the blockchain:

"Blind Signatures for Untraceable Payments" published by David Chaum in 1998:
www.bit.ly/blindsignatures

Digi-cash press release 27 May 1994 titled
"World's first electronic cash payment over computer networks."
www.bit.ly/DigiCashPress

Wei Dai's proposal for "b-money" in 1998:
www.weidai.com/bmoney.txt

Nick Szabo's website and post about bit gold, republished in 2008:
www.bit.ly/NickBitGold

Ethereum and smart contracts:
Ethereum foundation website:
www.ethereum.org/

Ethereum source code on GitHub:
www.github.com/ethereum/

Solidity programming language for creating smart contracts on the
Ethereum Virtual Machine:
www.solidity.readthedocs.io/en/develop/

Cryptocurrencies:

List of the largest cryptocurrencies by market capitalization:
www.coinmarketcap.com/

Coinbase – one of the largest web wallet companies to buy and sell
cryptocurrencies.
Note: Referral link below includes $10 free bitcoin after buying or
selling over $100 worth of bitcoins.
www.bit.ly/10freebitcoin

Bitcoin Blockchain explorers:

Blockchain.info:
www.blockchain.info/

Blockr:
www.btc.blockr.io/

Bitcoin Developer resources:
www.bitcoin.org/en/development

Glossary of Terms

Bitcoin (Uppercase B)
Bitcoin with an uppercase 'B' refers to the cryptocurrency payment network, protocols and blockchain.
As a protocol, Bitcoin is a set of rules that every client must follow to accept transactions and have its own transactions accepted by other clients.

As a network, Bitcoin is all the computers that follow the same rules and exchange transactions and blocks between each other.

Transactions are processed by the computers on the network between each other (Peer To Peer, P2P), there is no central bank, government or authority for issuing or managing transactions.

bitcoin (Lowercase b)
When the word bitcoin has a lowercase 'b' it is generally referring to units of bitcoin, for example "sending 0.5 bitcoins".
The total number of bitcoins will be limited to 21 million.

Block
A block is record on the blockchain that contains data about transactions and information to verify is a valid part of the blockchain.

Blocks contain a block header, transactions, timestamp, proof-of-work, a record of previous block and new transactions that have not yet been recorded on the blockchain.

A block permanently records the transactions and data it contains onto the blockchain. Each block contains information about the previous block, creating a chain linking the blocks.

"Proof-of-work" is a difficult to solve mathematical puzzle that is unique to that block. The puzzle is difficult to solve but easy to verify once it is solved. New blocks can't be submitted to the blockchain unless they contain the correct answer to this puzzle.

Mining is the process of solving the problem to submit a valid block to the blockchain. Miners are rewarded for solving this problem and submitting a valid block as incentive to contribute computing power and resources to the blockchain network.

On the Bitcoin blockchain a new block of transactions is added around every 10 minutes.

Block Height
Block Height is the number of blocks connected to that block on the blockchain.

A Block Height of 0 refers to the very first block, known as the "genesis block" on the blockchain. A Block Height of 1 refers to the block after the "genesis block" with each block added on top having a block height 1 number higher than the block before it.

Block Reward
Block reward is given to the miner that successfully processes a transaction and hashes a transaction block.

The reward is generally a fraction of the cryptocurrency paid to the miner. This reward depends on the cryptocurrency and varies with the difficult increasing and the block reward decreasing over time.

By providing rewards to miners, it encourages people to contribute computing power to the network, increasing security and reducing processing times, creating a faster more secure network.

Blockchain
A shared, public, distributed ledger of all confirmed transactions. A block contains a set of transactions that have been recently confirmed, it also contains a reference to the previous block before it.

By referencing the previous block, the blocks are linked together, creating a chain.

Anybody with access can view the transactions and blocks on the blockchain back to the first block, known as the genesis block.

A blockchain is updated by mining blocks with new transactions. Unconfirmed transactions are not part of the blockchain.

BTC
The most popular currency code for 1 Bitcoin. This is like "USD" for U.S Dollars or other common currency codes.

Confirmed Transaction
A confirmed transaction is a transaction that has been processed, verified by the network and included in the blockchain.

This is done through mining or proof-of-work in cryptocurrency networks such as Bitcoin.

Once a transaction is confirmed, it is unlikely to be reversed, however the confirmation number will determine the change of a transaction being rejected or reversed. See Confirmation Number.

Confirmation Number
Confirmation number is a measure of probability that transaction could be rejected from the main chain.

"Zero confirmations" means that transaction is unconfirmed (not in any block yet). One confirmation means that the transaction is included in the latest block in the main chain.

Two confirmations mean the transaction is included in the block right before the latest one. The probability of transaction being reversed ("double spent") is reduced exponentially as more blocks are added "on top" of it.

Consortium blockchain
A consortium blockchain is in between a private and public blockchain, it is partially decentralized but verification of the blocks is completed by a select group of miners.

A consortium blockchain allows private and efficient transactions without providing full control to one company or individual.

Cryptocurrency
A cryptocurrency is a type of digital currency that is not issued by a government, central bank or authority.

It is a combination of the words cryptography and currency as cryptocurrencies are created and operate using mathematics and encryption techniques.

Cryptographic Hash Function
A cryptographic hash function is an encryption method that hides data in a way that makes it almost impossible to decrypt without authorization.

A computer algorithm which takes any length or amount of input data and produces a fixed length output, known as the data's "hash." It can be used to easily verify that data has not been altered. Regardless of the input size or message length the output will always have the same output length. A small change in the input will result in a completely different output and hash value.

The hash is seemingly random and so it is prohibitively difficult to try to produce a specific hash by changing the data that is being hashed.

Cryptography
Cryptography is a field of mathematics focusing on encryption, security and data protection. Cryptography is the basis of cryptocurrencies that allows the creation, management and security of the networks to operate.

dApps (Decentralized Applications)
Decentralized Applications are applications that are open source, not controlled by one person or entity and run across a distributed blockchain or network of computers.

dApps have no central server, the users connect to each other through peer to peer connections.

Difficulty
Difficulty is a measure of how difficult it is to verify new blocks in a blockchain network.

With Bitcoin, it is a maximum target divided by the current target. Bitcoin difficult is adjusted every 2,016 based on the time taken to verify the previous 2,016 blocks.

Difficulty is adjusted to ensure verification of each block is kept to an interval of around 10 minutes.

At the time of writing the current bitcoin difficulty is 520,808,749,422 and is expected to increase by between 3-5% every two weeks.

Depth
Depth refers to a place in the blockchain. A transaction with 6 confirmations can also be called "6 blocks deep".

The greater the depth of a transaction in the blockchain the greater the reliability and trust of that transaction.

Double Spending
Double spending is where the same money is spent twice. If you have 5 bitcoins in your wallet and you send 5 bitcoins to one person, then immediately afterwards you send those same 5 bitcoins to another person, this is an attempt at double spending.

The Bitcoin network makes double spending very difficult as the network will detect both transactions, then reach consensus about which of the transactions to confirm and which to reject.

Only one of the transactions will be included in the blockchain and be considered valid.

The more confirmations (depth) a transaction has, the more difficult it is to double spend it.

A 51% attack is a scenario where double spend transactions could occur and the blockchain could be manipulated. See 51% attack.

Ether

Ether is a cryptocurrency that is used on the Ethereum network. It is used as payments for running distributed applications (dApps) on the Ethereum network.

The cryptocurrency Ether is the second largest cryptocurrency by market cap after Bitcoin with a market cap over $10 billion dollars.

Ethereum

Ethereum is a platform that allows distributed, decentralized applications such as smart contracts to run on a virtual machine on top of a blockchain network.

The Ethereum network uses the cryptocurrency Ether which acts as currency on the network. Ether is exchanged as payment for running decentralized apps on the network.

Genesis Block

A genesis block is the very block on a blockchain with no previous block before it.
In the Bitcoin blockchain the first block or "Genesis Block" was on the 3rd of January 2009 and contains a newspaper quote in its coinbase:
"The Times 03/Jan/2009 Chancellor on brink of second bailout for banks"
as a proof that there are no secretly pre-mined blocks to overtake the blockchain in the future.

The message ironically refers to a reason for the existence of Bitcoin: a constant inflation of money supply by governments and banks.

Ledger (Distributed)

A distributed ledger is database that that is spread across different computer systems, countries or organisations.
Records are stored one after the other in a continuous ledger.
Distributed ledger data can be either "permissioned" or "un-permissioned".
See Ledger (Permissioned) and Ledger (Un-permissioned)

Ledger (Permissioned)
A permissioned ledger is a ledger where permission is required to access the ledger.
There may be one owner or multiple owners of a permissioned ledger.
When new records are added to the ledger it is checked and confirmed by those with access.
A permissioned ledger may be used by governments or banks where the data is confidential. A shared permissioned ledger is faster than using an un-permissioned ledger while still providing verified data blocks with digital signatures that can be seen by all those with permission.

Ledger (Un-permissioned)
Un-permissioned ledgers are not owned by any person or entity. Anybody can add data to the ledger and everybody with access has exact copies of the ledger.

This creates protection from fraud or un-authorised entries being added as everybody with access must verify entries to the ledger, continually reach consensus on the ledger and maintain the integrity of the ledger.

Bitcoin is an example of an un-permissioned ledger.

Main Chain
The main chain is the main blockchain, it is the longest series of blocks that go back to the genesis block from the current block.

Mining

Mining is when computing power is used to solve mathematical problems that allows transactions to be verified and transaction blocks to be added to the blockchain.

Miners contribute computing power and resources such as electricity to the blockchain network that is used to confirm transactions and as a result they are rewarded for verifying a block with transaction fees and block rewards. New cryptocurrency coins are created through this process so it is viewed as mining them out of the network.

Bitcoin mining is the process of using computer hardware to do mathematical calculations for the Bitcoin network to confirm transactions. Miners collect transaction fees for the transactions they confirm and are awarded bitcoins for each block they verify.

Nonce

Stands for "number used once". A number in a block header which is continually changed to find a nonce that creates a valid hash during a search for proof-of-work. Each time the nonce is changed, the hash of the block header is recalculated.

Peer-to-Peer (P2P)

Peer-to-peer (P2P) is s system where participants on a network interact with each other directly without needing to go through a centralized system or intermediary.

Private Blockchains

Private blockchains are where the permission and access is owned by one central organization.

This could be for governments, banks and other institutions where the data contained in the blockchain is confidential and restricted.

Almost every organization and government already has private databases and systems. A private blockchain may be used in the same manner as a private internal database.

Public Blockchains

A public blockchain is a blockchain that allows access to anyone. Anybody can access the blockchain, transact, verify transactions and decide which blocks are added to the blockchain.

Bitcoin is an example of public blockchain, public blockchains are also generally referred to as decentralized blockchains.

Private Key

A private key is a code or data that provides you access to a wallet containing cryptocurrency.

Just like a PIN code gives you access to the money in your bank account when combined with your bank card, a private key gives you access to the money in your cryptocurrency wallet.

You should keep your private key a secret the same way you would your PIN code and not share it with anyone otherwise they will have access to your money.

Public Key

A public key is like your bank account number. When you combine the public key and the private key you can access the funds in your wallet.
You can share your public key to receive money into that wallet, however to access the wallet, you need to pair it with a private key.

Proof-of-Work (PoW)

Proof-of-work is a solution to mathematical puzzle that must be provided to add a block into the blockchain.

The puzzle is difficult to solve but easy to verify, like a combination to a lock. It is hard to guess the combination to a lock, but once the combination is known, it is easy for other people to use that combination and check it is the right combination for that lock.

With cryptocurrencies, it takes a large amount of computing power and resources to produce proof-of-work.

In Bitcoin, proof-of-work is a hash of a block header. A block is considered valid only if its hash is lower than the current target. Each block refers to a previous block thus accumulating previous proof-of-work and forming a blockchain.

Proof of Authority(PoA)

Proof-of-Authority is an alternative to proof-of-stake and proof-of-work. It provides decision making power to one of multiple clients on the database that have specific private keys allowing them to create transactions and blocks on the blockchain.

Proof-of-Stake
Proof-of-stake is an alternative to the proof-of-work and proof-of-authority systems.

Proof-of-stake is a process where the amount held in a cryptocurrency determines the amount that can be mined by the holder. A person that holds 5% of a cryptocurrency can mine 5% of the blocks.

There is a lot of computing power and resources that goes towards mining and the proof-of-work process only to prove that resources were contributed to mining a block.

Proof-of-stake goes on the assumption the people with a stake in the cryptocurrency will not want to devalue their holdings so will act in their best interests of the network while saving computing power and resources.

Peercoin was the first cryptocurrency to use proof-of-Stake.

Satoshi
A Satoshi is the smallest amount of Bitcoin. 1 Satoshi is equal to 0.00000001 of a bitcoin.
The name Satoshi is in honor of the creator of Bitcoin Satoshi Nakamoto.

Satoshi Nakamoto
Satoshi Nakamoto is the name of the anonymous creator of Bitcoin. Nobody is yet certain if this is one person or a group of people. There is a lot of theories about who and how many people worked on Bitcoin, of which nationality or age, but no one has any evidence about their identity.

At the time of writing the identity of Satoshi Nakamoto is still a mystery.

SHA (Secure Hash Algorithm)

Secure Hash Algorithms are a type cryptographic hash functions created by the National Institute of Standards and Technology (NIST) as a U.S. Federal Information Processing Standard (FIPS).

The Secure Hash Algorithms are one way meaning that once data has been encrypted it is almost impossible for anyone without access to decrypt it.
See "Cryptographic Hash Function", "SHA 256"

SHA 256

SHA 256 is a Secure Hash Algorithm used in Bitcoin's proof-of-work system.
The SHA-256 algorithm generates unique, fixed-size 256-bit (32-byte) hash.

Signature

A signature in cryptocurrencies is a mathematical way to prove ownership and authority to access funds and conduct transactions.

With Bitcoin, a private key must match a public key to sign a transaction. The Bitcoin network can verify that the private key and public match on a signature for a transaction but the private key remains hidden from the network.

Bitcoin uses Elliptic Curve Digital Signature Algorithm (ECDSA) for signing transactions.

Smart Contracts

Smart contracts are contracts that are written in computer code and operate on a blockchain or distributed ledger.

They automatically verify, execute and enforce the contract based on the terms written in the code.

Smart contracts can be partially or fully self-executing and self-enforcing.

Solidity
Solidity is a programming language used for programming code compiled by the Ethereum Virtual Machine, to be used in smart contracts or decentralized apps (dApps) on the Ethereum network. It has a syntax structure like JavaScript.

Unconfirmed Transaction
Transaction that is not included in any block. Also known as "0-confirmation" transaction. Unconfirmed transactions will remain unconfirmed until the network decides to throw it away, find it in the blockchain, or include it in the blockchain itself. See also Confirmation Number.

51% Attack
A 51% attack, is also known a more than 50% attack or a double spend attack. This occurs if more than 50% of the computing power on a cryptocurrency network is controlled by one person or group of people working together.

By controlling more than 50% of the computing power on a network, they can alter the network and blockchain allowing double spending, manipulating transactions and preventing transactions from being confirmed.

While possible in theory, the more miners and computing power on a network the more difficult a 51% attack becomes.

A 51% attack is highly unlikely on the bitcoin network, but more possible on smaller, newly established cryptocurrencies.

About
This glossary of terms is based on work by Oleg Andreev.

About the Author

Mark Gates grew up in California and has been a part of the tech scene for over a decade.

He started designing web sites while still in high school using HTML and plain text in a notepad before advanced tools existed. Mark started a web design business in college during the start of the Internet boom over 15 years ago.

Mark expanded his web design business into digital marketing, SEO and social media. After selling his business, he currently spends his time traveling the world making money from his laptop.

While first sceptical about cryptocurrencies, Mark has become a become a strong proponent of blockchain based-technologies and cryptocurrencies.

Mark believes that the best way to learn is with real world experience. He loves delving into anything tech related, getting hands on knowledge and teaching others to do the same.

Whether you're launching a website, marketing an existing business, trading cryptocurrencies, learning programming or looking for real world skills to land you a dream job. Mark writes his books with easy to understand language and practical exercises designed to get you to your goal.

Even if you have no previous experience, Mark's books will take you from beginner to tech-master in no time.

Other books by Mark Gates can be found on Amazon.

Errors and Feedback

Please Contact Us If You Find Any Errors

While every effort is taken to ensure the quality and accuracy of this book. Spelling, grammar and other errors are often missed in the early versions of publication.

We appreciate you contacting us first if you noticed any errors in this book before taking any other action. This allows us to quickly fix these errors before it negatively impacts the author.

If you find any issues or errors with this book, please contact us and we'll correct these as soon as possible.

Readers that notify us of errors will be invited to receive advance reader copies of future books published.

Errors: errors@wisefoxpub.com

Feedback

For any general feedback about the book, please feel free to contact us at the email address below:

Feedback: contact@wisefoxpub.com